Caring for Our Elders

Caring for Our Elders

MULTICULTURAL EXPERIENCES
with NURSING HOME PLACEMENT

Patricia J. Kolb

Columbia University Press

New York

COLUMBIA UNIVERSITY PRESS

Publishers Since 1893

New York   Chichester, West Sussex

© 2003 Columbia University Press

All rights reserved

Library of Congress Cataloging-in-Publication Data

Kolb, Patricia J.

Caring for our elders : multicultural experiences with

nursing home placement / Patricia J. Kolb.

p.   cm.

Includes bibliographical references and index.

ISBN 0-231-11458-3 (cl. : alk. paper) — ISBN 0-231-11459-1 (pbk. : alk. paper)

1. Aged—Nursing home care—United States.   2. Minority aged—Nursing home

care—United States.   3. Caregivers.   I. Title.

RC954.3.K65 2003

362.1'6'0973–dc21

2003043401

∞

Columbia University Press books are printed on permanent

and durable acid-free paper.

Printed in the United States of America

c 10 9 8 7 6 5 4 3 2 1

p 10 9 8 7 6 5 4 3 2 1

Dedication

For Anthony

———•———

For nursing home residents
For devoted relatives and friends
of nursing home residents

———•———

In memory of Dr. Stanford M. Lyman, sociologist,
professor, scholar, author, and mentor

CONTENTS

ACKNOWLEDGMENTS

I AM PLEASED to have the opportunity to acknowledge the contributions of people who have been especially helpful in the development of this book. I am extremely grateful to the caregiving relatives and friends who agreed to be interviewed for this exploration of nursing home placement and who shared their experiences so thoroughly. They have my respect and admiration for their dedication and their ability and desire to remain caregivers even when confronted with incredibly difficult circumstances.

I am very grateful to the staff at the nursing home for allowing me to carry out this study and for giving me valuable opportunities to learn about and provide nursing home social work services and to supervise many fine graduate students.

I am also grateful to former colleagues at the Columbia University School of Social Work who have been so supportive of my work on this project. I thank Dr. Gary Mallon for suggesting that information from my research study could be published as a book and for advising me on approaches to beginning that process. Dr. Barbara Simon also provided strong support for publication of this book. Ms. Janet Abbott understood the importance of this subject and has been a source of consistent support. Finally, I want to thank Dr. Peg McCartt Hess, who, as Associate Dean of the Columbia University School of Social Work, steadfastly believed in and nurtured my ability to succeed as an academician and contributed in important ways to my being able to write this book.

My colleagues in the Social Work Program at Lehman College, City University of New York, have provided valuable support for my long-standing commitment to geriatrics/gerontology through their strong participation in our Council on Social Work Education–John A. Hartford Foundation curriculum development project.

I am very grateful to Mr. John L. Michel, senior executive editor at Columbia University Press, for his editorial assistance and appreciation of the complexities and importance of caregiving, and I appreciate the thoughtful contributions of the readers who provided recommendations to me.

I am especially appreciative of the patience and understanding that I received from my son, Anthony Torchio, as I spent many, many long hours writing this book. Thank you very much, Anthony. You are a very special son.

Caring for Our Elders

INTRODUCTION

THE NUMBER OF PEOPLE age sixty-five and over in the United States increased dramatically during the 1900s as life expectancy at birth rose from forty-seven years in 1900 to more than seventy years by the end of the century. Affecting each of us personally in our families and communities, a demographic explosion is taking place; the number of older adults will become larger and more diverse ethnically and racially in the twenty-first century. The number of people age sixty-five and over is projected to increase from about 34 million in the late 1990s to 80 million by 2050. The most rapidly growing proportion of the population, those age eighty-five and over, is expected to increase fivefold between 1996 and 2050. The phenomenon of a rapidly increasing older adult population is not limited to the United States; it is part of an unprecedented change that is occurring throughout the world.

Relatives and friends continue to provide the majority of assistance to older adults, but major societal changes since the 1970s have resulted in alterations in caregiving for this age group in the United States and other industrialized countries. In addition to increased life expectancy, more women are engaged in paid employment outside the home and more marriages are ending in divorce, two other developments that have contributed to changes in the family and other social institutions.

A reality of modern life is that older adults and their families often find that care provided by family and friends, even when supplemented by home care from paid caregivers, is inadequate to meet their needs. Although many dread nursing home placement, the changes in life expectancy and the lack of availability of family members to serve as caregivers have meant that more people are turning to nursing homes to provide the necessary care. Almost 40 percent of all people age sixty-five and over in the United States spend some time in a nursing home, although only 5 percent are in such a facility at any specific time. Members of ethnically and racially diverse families that have not used nursing homes in the past now are doing so.

Despite these changes, very little has been written about family caregiving for nursing home residents or about nursing home placement for those who belong to diverse racial and ethnic groups. The assumption has often been that nursing home placement *never* occurs within groups that have a strong tradition of filial piety, implying that it is unnecessary to consider emotional and informational needs, to explore service delivery issues, or to design research studies focusing on families of diverse backgrounds who are experiencing nursing home placement.

My interest in developing greater understanding of the experiences of nursing home residents and their families from diverse racial and ethnic backgrounds began while I was employed as a social worker at Acacia Nursing Home,[*] the facility where I carried out the research study on which this book is based. As I came to appreciate the uniqueness of the experiences of each resident and his or her relatives and friends whom I met there, I began to learn about the effects of cultural heritage and history related to ethnicity and race on these families' experiences. Understanding the meaning of nursing home placement from the perspective of family members' values and role expectations pertaining to later adulthood was important to me as a social worker. With increased awareness, I became convinced that service providers from all disciplines engaged in working in nursing homes need a well-informed understanding of the cultural traditions and expectations of each individual as shaped by his or her socialization. Openness to learning about these traditions and expectations directly from nursing home residents and their informal caregivers is essential, and my goal in this book is to impart information that will supplement your efforts to learn directly from the older adults and their caregivers whom you know. It is my hope that the information presented here will increase understanding of the diversity of aging and caregiving experiences and contribute to the provision of culturally sensitive services.

---

[*]Acacia Nursing Home is a fictitious name for a large Jewish nursing home located in a city in the northeastern United States.

This book describes the experiences of seventy-five African American and Afro-Caribbean, white Jewish, and Latina/o residents and the relatives and friends who have been their caregivers. The residents lived in Acacia Nursing Home, a large facility located in an urban area in the northeastern United States. Although Acacia is a Jewish social welfare institution, the residents are very diverse racially, ethnically, and spiritually.

When I was employed as a social worker at Acacia Nursing Home, I learned that a nursing home is a dynamic community filled with individuals possessing strength and courage who live there, work there, and visit. Every day residents socially construct their realities according to many factors: previously learned knowledge and skills; current experiences, opportunities, and aspirations; and relationships with formal (paid) and informal (unpaid) caregivers. Each individual, therefore, views reality through a different experiential lens. When I began to know staff members and the residents and their relatives and friends as individuals, my appreciation of their individuality increased. I no longer viewed the residents sitting along the hallway of a nursing home floor as a group of nearly indistinguishable individuals; they seemed almost magically transformed into individuals with unique personalities and assortments of characteristics forged throughout their lives. As a social worker, I needed to relate to them with this understanding.

I decided to conduct an exploratory study to learn more about the experiences of residents and the informal caregivers, relatives, and friends who continued to be involved in their lives. I wanted to address the lack of research information about nursing home placement among ethnically and racially diverse families, processes of nursing home placement and adjustment, and informal caregiving provided to nursing home residents. Before I interviewed the primary informal caregivers, I did not know in any systematic way whether the experiences of residents and their relatives were influenced by broad social changes; my developing awareness of the significance of that influence resulted from analysis of the content of the interviews.

The study used semistructured interviews to obtain information about residents' relationships earlier in their lives, the placement process, and experiences of the residents and their families and friends after the residents' admission. I developed an interview guide in which many of the questions were open-ended, because I approached the study knowing that it was impossible to predict the participants' responses and that it was important to hear about each person's experiences and emotions in his or her own words.

More than one selection method was employed to choose the research sample, since the resident population in each group (African American and Afro-Caribbean, Jewish, and Latina/o) varied greatly as a proportion of the total population of the nursing home. The relatives or friends of twenty-five residents in each group who were interviewed were usually the primary contact people whose names were listed in the records.

To ensure objectivity in the selection process, in April 1995 I asked the social workers at the nursing home to give me a list of the Latino residents. They provided the names of 27 residents, who occupied 5 percent of the beds, and the primary contact person in each family. Other Latino residents were added to the list as more were admitted. The Jewish participants were determined in February 1996 from a computer-generated list of 320 residents (who occupied 62 percent of the beds) by selecting every eleventh name (listed consecutively by room number on each floor), to ensure that residents from each of the long-term floors would be included. In January 1997 a computer-generated list of the 69 African American and Afro-Caribbean residents (who occupied 13 percent of the beds) was obtained and arranged alphabetically by floor to ensure the selection of participants from all floors. The names of residents whose caregivers would be contacted for interviews were then determined by choosing the first two names alphabetically for each floor and moving on to the next name for that floor if it was not possible to interview the caregiver of a resident who was initially selected.

The residents' case records provided supplementary demographic and diagnostic information, including date and place of birth, date of migration from Puerto Rico or immigration from other countries, employment history, interests before admission, marital status, and primary language. The records also identified home care arrangements and previous residence, as well as diagnoses at the time of admission.

This book is unique in several ways. In addition to describing the experiences of residents and their relatives and friends of diverse racial and ethnic backgrounds, it describes nursing home placement within the larger framework of the residents' relationships and other experiences before the onset of declining health and throughout their adjustment to Acacia Nursing Home. Applying Drachman and Ryan's (1991) stage-of-migration framework to the process of nursing home placement, experiences of residents and their relatives and friends are conceptualized as a three-stage process: premigration and departure from home, migration, and resettlement.

I chose to refer to the nursing home that welcomed the residents as Acacia to represent it as a place where strength, survival, and growth abound in challenging terrain. Nursing home residents, staff, relatives and friends of residents, and volunteers constantly marshal their very considerable resources to meet the demands of each day within a larger social environment in which nursing homes tend to be devalued, understaffed, and underfunded. Since the development of the additional programs needed in communities to provide alternatives to nursing home placement for older adults is lagging, it is likely that the need for nursing home care provided by caring and committed staff will continue to increase.

You will come to know the residents, their caregivers, and their individual experiences as you read this book, and this knowledge will provide new insights into the experiences of families as they participate in the process of nursing home placement. Chapter 1, "The Need for Nursing Home Placement," briefly describes relevant demographic changes and changes in families in the United States, as well as sociological perspectives that facilitate our understanding of individuals within the context of larger social environments and the experiences of people who have been marginalized. Matilda White Riley's concept of social change and the life course is introduced as a useful approach for understanding differences in the aging experience in different time periods. Chapter 2, "Research About Caregiving by Family and Friends," reviews published information about informal caregiving, which is relevant to the experiences of the families in this study, and begins to relate this information to the experiences of caregivers in the Acacia Nursing Home study. Subjects that are addressed include tasks performed; motivation for caregiving; emotional responses to caregiving; gender, ethnicity, and caregiving; and ethnicity and nursing home placement.

Chapter 3, "Earlier Years: Life Within Families and Communities," describes life before the need for assistance developed, identifying the beginning of a premigration period for the future residents and their caregivers, applying Drachman and Ryan's stage-of-migration framework to the nursing home placement process. Areas of exploration include family relationships, parenting and grandparenting, independence of some people who later became residents, participation in communities, and immigration and migration. Chapter 4, "Changing Health, Changing Relationships," identifies diseases that developed in some of the older adults and the changes within families as some of their elders began to need assistance at home. The role of formal home care providers in providing assistance is also described.

Chapter 5, "The Placement Process: Decisions and Transitions," addresses the complex issues involved at the beginning of the transit stage of nursing home placement, the process of deciding that nursing home placement is needed. Chapter 6, "Settling In: Adjusting to the Changes," continues the discussion of the transit process by describing what admission day was like for the Acacia Nursing Home residents in the study and their caregivers. The chapter also introduces the next stage, resettlement, which involves adjustment to nursing home life. Chapter 7, "Continuing to Care for Relatives in the Nursing Home," further explores resettlement, examining the continued participation of relatives and friends in caregiving. And finally chapter 8, "Who Helps Residents and Their Relatives?," addresses the roles of formal service providers in nursing homes and describes characteristics of the systems in which they work.

1

THE NEED FOR
NURSING HOME PLACEMENT

She had a couple of falls at home, and we didn't know what was happening. Then, all of a sudden her level of consciousness just totally changed. We did not know what was happening with her, and we hired someone to come in and stay with her because she was really confused, and she was changing rapidly. A physician I know offered to come to her house and see her. He thought she needed to be admitted to the hospital, and he came to her home and said we definitely need to admit her. Before her level of consciousness changed, she said she didn't want to go to the emergency room, so this doctor admitted her to the hospital and she didn't need to go to the emergency room. She was seen by a neurologist who said that she had a hematoma, partly old, partly new. It had filled up so much of the cranial space by now that we were seeing the symptoms, but it could have been happening for years. They had to go in and evacuate, and once they evacuated it, she lost a lot of her functioning and we just knew that she could never go back home and live alone again. In fact, before this happened, we actually wanted her to have a home health aide and she totally refused. I mean she was 92 . . . like, ma!

—A resident's daughter, two years after her mother's admission to the nursing home

WHILE SOME OLDER PEOPLE in the United States are able to live independently until the end of their lives, many, like the woman described above, eventually move to a nursing home. We need to understand all the factors, including contemporary social changes, that contribute to the need for nursing home placement. This chapter focuses primarily on two significant changes that are reflected in the decisions for placement made by many of the families in this study: extended life expectancy and employment outside of the home for greater numbers of women, who have traditionally been the primary caregivers.

THE "GERONTOLOGICAL EXPLOSION"

The twentieth century saw a dramatic increase in life expectancy in the United States. In 1900 life expectancy at birth was 47 years; by 2002 it had increased to nearly 77 years (Moody 2002). According to the U.S.

Bureau of the Census, the number of people age 65 and over increased from 3.1 million in 1900 to 33.9 million in 1996, and is projected to reach 80 million by 2050 (U.S. Bureau of the Census 1996, 1997). Those who are age 85 and over constitute the most rapidly growing group; it is projected that this oldest cohort will account for nearly 5 percent of the nation's population by the middle of the twenty-first century (U.S. Bureau of the Census 1996, 1997). In 1996 the U.S. population included 3.8 million people 85 and over, and the Census Bureau projects that in 2050 that number will have increased to 18.9 million (U.S. Bureau of the Census 1996, 1997).

The U.S. Bureau of the Census predicts a larger population of older people who belong to ethnic and racial minority groups and also predicts that older people will become a larger proportion of their own ethnic and racial groups. These changes within the United States reflect the trend toward worldwide increases in the numbers and in the proportion of older people in the populations of developed and developing countries. Projected increases globally are related to the high rates of fertility that followed World War II, as well as to reductions in the death rate at all ages, in infectious and parasitic diseases, and in infant and maternal mortality; improved nutrition; and improvements in health services, education, and income (U.S. Bureau of the Census 1993).

While the general trend in the United States is toward increased life expectancy, variations exist among racial and ethnic groups. Differences and commonalities across groups are indicated in recent census data, but the data are limited because the Bureau of the Census does not prepare projections based upon national origin. It does make projections for racial groups and for people of Hispanic origin. Projections are based upon assumptions about fertility, mortality, and net immigration (Angel and Hogan 1994).

The Bureau of the Census report *65+ in the United States* cites the following trends:

- The elderly population increased 11-fold from 1900 to 1994, compared with only a 3-fold increase for those under age 65. Elderly population growth rates for the 1990–2010 period will be modest, but during the 2010–2030 period, elderly growth rates will increase dramatically as the Baby Boom generation ages into the 65 and over group.
- From 1960 to 1994, the oldest old population (persons aged 85 and over) increased by 274 percent, compared with 100 percent for the

65 and over, and 45 percent for the total population. The oldest old population in 1994 would more than double to 7 million in 2020 under middle series projections.

- The oldest old would reach 19 million by 2050, or as many as 27 million under the Census Bureau's "highest series" assumptions of future life expectancy and net immigration.
- Racial and ethnic diversity within the elderly population will continue to increase. The proportion of the elderly that is white, non-Hispanic is projected to decline from 87 percent in 1990 to 67 percent in 2050. Among the elderly in 2050, 10 percent would be black, non-Hispanic; 7 percent Asian and Pacific Islander, non-Hispanic; less than 1 percent American Indian, Eskimo, and Aleut, non-Hispanic; and 16 percent Hispanic.
- Among elderly blacks and Hispanics, about 1 in 5 were 80 years or older in 1990. By 2050, these proportions could increase to 30 percent for elderly blacks and 36 percent for elderly Hispanics. The proportion aged 80 years and over among elderly whites would be even higher (40 percent).
- Income and poverty differences are significant in population subgroups. Elderly white men had higher median incomes in 1992 than other population subgroups of the elderly. The 1992 poverty rates were higher for elderly blacks (33 percent) and Hispanics (22 percent) than for whites (11 percent).
- Gender and life expectancy rates at birth persist. Life expectancy at birth in 1991 was about 80 years for white females, 74 years for black females, 73 years for white males, and 65 years for black males.
- Elderly women are less likely than men to live in a family setting. After age 75, most women are widowed and live alone, while most men are married and live with their wives.
- Women's share of the older labor force (55 years and over) increased from 23 percent in 1950 to 44 percent in 1993.
- Elderly women (16 percent) were more likely to be poor in 1992 than elderly men (9 percent). Of the 2.3 million elderly poor who lived alone in 1992, 2.0 million were women.
- Noninstitutionalized elderly persons reporting the need for personal assistance with everyday activities in 1990–91 increased with age, from only 9 percent of persons aged 65 to 69 up to 50 percent of the oldest old.

• As average length of life continues to increase, issues regarding the quality of extended life (active life expectancy) are likely to assume greater importance.   (U.S. Bureau of the Census 1996:v–vii)

Using census data, Angel and Hogan have addressed issues regarding "the gerontological explosion." They suggest that the study of older persons in the United States has been a study of older whites, who were a large majority of the older population, but that the demographic realities are changing rapidly. Stating that over the next fifty years the number of older people in ethnic minority groups is projected to increase more rapidly than the number of older people who are white, they discuss the factors that influence demographic processes over time. They suggest that the mortality and migration experiences of members of minority groups in this country have differed from these processes in the white population. Mortality is generally higher for members of racial and ethnic minority groups, including people who are American Indian, black, and Mexican American, but some groups, such as Japanese Americans, do exhibit lower mortality. International migration has had a much greater effect on the size of the Cuban, Mexican, and Puerto Rican populations and some Asian groups in this country than on other groups (Angel and Hogan 1994).

"SHIFTING THE CENTER"

It is apparent from demographic data and from the results of the study at Acacia Nursing Home that discussion of the relationships among changes in society, the care of older people, and the needs of their familial caregivers must address the experiences of people of diverse racial and ethnic backgrounds. It is time to "shift the center" when discussing the need for nursing home placement and include older people and their families of all backgrounds. In developing the concept of shifting the center, Andersen and Collins have said:

"Shifting the center" means putting at the center of our thinking the experiences of groups who have formerly been excluded. Without doing so, many groups simply remain invisible. When they are seen, they are typically judged through experiences of White people, rather than understood on their own terms; this establishes a false norm through which all groups are judged. . . . Thinking more inclusively

opens up the way the world is viewed, making the experience of previously excluded groups more visible and central in the construction
of knowledge. Inclusive thinking shifts our perspective from the
white, male-centered forms of thinking that have characterized much
of Western thought, helping us better understand the intersections of
race, class, and gender in the experiences of all groups, including
those with privilege and power.   (Andersen and Collins 2001:14–15)

Andersen and Collins tell us that reconstruction of knowledge matters
because learning about other groups helps members of both the dominant
and the subordinate groups to understand the partiality of their own perspective. Furthermore, they add that misleading and incorrect knowledge
results in poor social analysis and bad social policy, "policy that then repro-
duces, rather than solves, social problems." Third, they remind us that
knowledge provides an orientation to the world, influencing how we be-
have and think about ourselves and others. Therefore, if what we know is
based on exclusionary thought and is wrong, we are likely to act in exclusionary ways (Andersen and Collins 2001:15).

While some research and professional literature addresses ethnicity and
nursing home placement among people whose ancestry is other than An-
glo, the information available to practitioners and academicians is still
quite limited. Keeping in mind the concept of "shifting the center," service providers and researchers need to examine the implications of the realities faced by increasing numbers of older people who are members of ethnic and racial minority groups, as well as the implications for older adults
who are white. The data on increased life expectancy among members of
racial and ethnic minority groups in this country are compelling. Projections from the year 2000 to 2025 for people 65 and over who are black,
Latino, and non-Hispanic white indicate that the number of non-Hispanic
black older people will increase from 2.8 million to 5.6 million (U.S. Bureau of the Census 1997). Among Latinos, the increase will be from 1.9
million to 6.1 million, and among whites, from 29.1 million to 47.3 million (U.S. Bureau of the Census 1997).

It is projected that by 2050 the number of people 65 and over who are
black will be 8.4 million, including an increase in those who are 85 and older from 0.2 million in 1990 to 1.4 million in the year 2050. As a percentage of the total number of people 65 and over in the United States, the black
population is projected to increase from 8 percent in 1990 to 10.4 percent
in 2050 (U.S. Bureau of the Census 1996).

The 65 and over Latino population is growing much faster than the black population in the same age group. The middle series projections predict 7.6 million Hispanic people in this age group in 2030, compared to 6.8 million black older adults. The number of people 65 and over is projected to reach 12.5 million in 2050, with an increase in the number of people 85 and over from 0.1 million in 1990 to 2.6 million in 2050 (U.S. Bureau of the Census 1996).

In 1989 the composition of the Latino population of people 65 and over, by nationality, was Mexican Americans, 48 percent; Cuban Americans, 18 percent; mainland Puerto Ricans, 11 percent; Central and South Americans, 8 percent; and other, 15 percent (Angel and Hogan 1994). In 1994 around 62 percent of Latinos who were 65 and over were in the 65–74 age group; by 2050 that figure is projected to decrease to less than 50 percent. The largest increase among Latinos 65 and over is projected to be in the 85-plus age group (Angel and Hogan 1994).

The American Indian, Eskimo, and Aleut populations that are 65 and over are projected to increase substantially from 2000 to 2025, from 149,000 to 320,000. Likewise, the number of people 85 and over in these groups is expected to increase from 21,000 to 52,000, or 1 percent to 1.9 percent.

The Asian and Pacific Islander population 65 and over is projected to increase from 782,000 in the year 2000 to 2.6 million in 2025, and the number of people 85 and over in this group, from 51,000 to 308,000, or 0.5 percent to 1.5 percent (U.S. Bureau of the Census 1997).

"PRIVATE TROUBLES" AND "PUBLIC ISSUES"

With life expectancy rising across a broad spectrum of groups in the United States, the care of older people has become a public issue that manifests itself in the lives of individuals in diverse ways. The events leading up to nursing home placement for one African American resident, described by her daughter at the beginning of this chapter, provide but one glimpse of one family facing this complex situation. C. Wright Mills's distinction between "private troubles" and "public issues" is useful for our analysis of demographic changes and their implications for the increased use of U.S. nursing homes:

Troubles occur within the character of the individual and within the range of his immediate relations with others; they have to do with his self and with those limited areas of social life of which he is directly and personally aware. Accordingly, the statement and the resolution of troubles properly lie within the individual as a biographical entity and within the scope of his immediate milieu—the social setting that is directly open to his personal experience and to some extent his willful activity. A trouble is a private matter; values cherished by an individual are felt by him to be threatened.

Issues have to do with matters that transcend these local environments of the individual and the range of his inner life. They have to do with the organization of many such milieux into the institutions of an historical society as a whole, with the ways in which various milieux overlap and interpenetrate to form the larger structure of social and historical life. An issue is a public matter; some value cherished by publics is felt to be threatened. Often there is a debate about what the value really is and about what it is that really threatens it. This debate is often without focus if only because it is the very nature of an issue, unlike even widespread trouble, that it cannot very well be defined in terms of the immediate and everyday environments of ordinary men. An issue, in fact, often involves a crisis in institutional arrangements, and often too it involves what Marxists call "contradictions" or "antagonisms." (Mills 1959:8–9)

The care of older people in need of assistance is a public issue with complex variations in the manner in which families and older people experience and address this need. Demographic data regarding the "gerontological explosion," statistics documenting the use of nursing homes, and my research data are all helpful in identifying some of the variables in individuals' experiences.

Statistical data clearly show that nursing home care is a resource that many older adults ultimately use. Although only about 5 percent, or 1.6 million, of all people over the age of 65 are in nursing homes at any given time, Moody has noted that up to 40 percent of those who reach age 65 will live in a nursing home at some time before they die. Moody refers to the error of citing 5 percent as the proportion of all people over 65 who will live in a nursing home as the 5 percent fallacy (Moody 2002:22).

Figures on the number of nursing home admissions and nursing home beds illustrate the increasing rate of placement, projecting that more than 4 million people will live in nursing homes by 2040 (Manton and Soldo 1985; Moody 2002). The number of nursing home admissions increased from 1.1 million in 1972 to 1.7 million in 1994. The National Center for Health and Statistics of the Centers for Disease Control (CDC) released data identifying 16,700 nursing homes with 1.77 million beds in 1995, an increase from 15,700 homes with 1.2 million beds in 1972. The 1995 distribution of residents was 72.3 percent female and 27.7 percent male; 35.8 percent were age 85 and over; and 88 percent of the residents were white, 9.7 percent black, and 1.7 percent other races, with the largest proportion of nonwhite nursing home residents living in the South and the West (Darnay 1998).

While the number and proportion of people in the United States who are living to more advanced ages have increased, another structural change has been happening simultaneously—the steadily increasing number of women who are engaged in paid employment. Labor force participation of women is an important variable in the need for nursing home placement, since employment can diminish availability for caregiving. The traditional expectation in many cultures that females will be the primary caregivers within their families has been addressed extensively in the literature (Abel 1991; Berg-Weger and Rubio 1995; Bumagin and Hirn 2001; Cancian and Oliker 2000; Eckert and Shulman 1996; Hagestad 2000; Kosberg 1992; Toseland and Smith 1991; Walter 1991).

In 1996 the U.S. Bureau of Labor Statistics reported a total of 53.2 million families that included a married couple. In 28.1 million of these families both the husband and the wife were employed, in 2.8 million only the wife was employed, and in 10.1 million only the husband was employed. In 3.4 million families, there were other employment combinations, and in 8,766 families no members were employed. Among families that did not include a married couple, 12.3 million were maintained by women. There was at least one employed person in 8.8 million of these, and in 5.0 million the householder was the only employed family member (U.S. Bureau of Labor Statistics 1998).

The trend toward paid employment for females is reflected in U.S. Bureau of Labor Statistics figures citing an 18 percent increase in labor force participation among women age 16 and over from 1986 to 1996 and a projected increase from 1996 to 2006 of 14.2 percent. Expressed in raw numbers, the 1986 figure of 52.4 million women in this age group participating in the civilian labor force is expected to increase to 70.6 million in 2006. These figures compare with the labor force participation of 65.4 million men age 16 and over in 1986, projected to increase to 78.2 million in 2006. The percentage increase for men from 1986 to 1996 was 10.2 percent, and the projected increase from 1996 to 2006 is 8.5 percent; the U.S. Bureau of Labor Statistics figures predict that women's proportion of the labor force will increase from the 44.5 percent 1986 figure to 47.4 percent in 2006 (U.S. Bureau of Labor Statistics 1997).

Marital disruption is an event that contributes to the necessity for many females to obtain paid employment. The increase in the number of divorces is documented by U.S. Bureau of the Census data on marital status of people age 15 and over. In 1970, 2.7 million women identified themselves as divorced; by 1997 the figure had increased to 11.1 million. During the same period, the number of men indicating that they were divorced increased substantially as well, from 1.6 million in 1970 to 6.2 million in 1997. The limited information available about racial differences indicates an increase in divorce for black females from 355,000 in 1970 to 1.6 million in 1997. For black males, the increase was from 212,000 to 1.0 million. The number of white females reported as divorced in 1970 was 2.3 million, which increased to 9.2 million in 1997. For white males, the number increased from 1.3 million to 6.9 million over the same period of time (U.S. Bureau of the Census 1997).

RILEY'S PARADIGM, SOCIAL CHANGE, AND NURSING HOME PLACEMENT

Demographic data clearly indicate that structural changes are affecting families on a large scale in the United States. With increasing longevity, a larger number of individuals eventually need assistance from informal or formal service providers, or both. The changes noted—more older people needing extensive assistance, more women in the labor force, and more divorces—make it difficult for families to provide sufficient care. As the daughter of the nursing home resident described in the quotation at the beginning of this chapter said, "I know that she requires a lot of care, and we all work and I don't think we'd be able to take care of her."

Matilda White Riley's conceptualization of social change and the life course helps us to understand the relationship between social changes occurring in the United States and the behavior of individuals within social institutions such as the family. The paradigm that she developed as an integral component of her sociology of age provides a useful tool for understanding the many layers of systems that influence the behavior of people who place themselves or relatives in a nursing home. It helps us to visualize the reciprocal relationship between macro- and micro-level systems, focusing upon the interaction between the lives of individuals and macro-level social changes. As Riley says, sociology of age "provides an analytical framework for understanding the interplay between human lives and changing social structures" (Riley 1987:1).

Riley's paradigm provides a diachronic view that shows the relationship between changing lives and changes in social structures. We can visualize the transactional relationships between individuals as they move through their lifespan, in which life expectancy for all cohorts within extended families is increasing, and their social environment, in which structural changes involving family roles, relationships, and composition are occurring within the institution of the family.

Components of Riley's approach include (1) the process of aging over the life course, (2) societies and groups that are stratified by age, and (3) the succession of cohorts that provide the link between individuals who are aging and societies and groups that are stratified by age (Riley 1987). Individuals are viewed as members of cohorts moving through their lifespan during different periods of time, creating changes in societies through participation in social institutions such as the family. According to Riley, age is a structural aspect of any changing society or group, and aging individuals and changes in society influence each other continuously (Riley 1987).

Riley rejects the idea that the life stages of individuals result solely from biological, or ontogenetic, development (Riley 1986). She proposes that they are the product of the interplay between aging, or development, and social change. Life stages are not fixed; they vary with social structure and social change. She suggests three principles:

1. In response to social change, people engage in new age-typical patterns and regularities of behavior (change in the way the aging process occurs);
2. As these behavior patterns become commonplace, they are defined as age-appropriate norms and rules, are reinforced by "authorities," and are thereby institutionalized in the role structure of society (change in the social structure);
3. In turn, these changes in age norms and social structures redirect or otherwise alter a panoply of age-related behaviors (further changes in the aging process); and so on.

(Riley and Riley 1986:55)

An understanding of the dynamics of aging of individuals within cohorts from the perspective of macro-level social changes can enable policymakers

in the field of aging, administrators in nursing homes, service providers at-
tempting to assist older people and their families, researchers, and older
people and their families to understand the salient variables in planning,
service delivery, and research. Although Riley's work is well known in the
field of gerontology, it is apparent that her paradigm and the sociology of
age are concerned with understanding the behavior of people of all ages and
can assist us in identifying the complexities of the issues that affect the lives
of caregivers of all ages.

Riley and Riley's description of structural lag illuminates another important issue in nursing home placement. While the Rileys approach structural lag in terms of the lack of resources for healthy older people, the concept
is also relevant to older people, like those in this study, who need extensive
personal care, skilled nursing care, and supervision. In addressing the issue
of structural lag, the Rileys state:

> As longevity increases, the complex processes of aging from birth to
> death—biological, psychological, and social—are continuously being
> shaped by ongoing changes in structure and social roles. Meanwhile,
> as the life course is modified, pressures are generated for still further
> changes—in social structures, institutions, beliefs, norms, and values.
> In turn, these societal changes influence the nature of the life course.
> Thus, there is a continuing dialectic between the processes of aging
> and changing social structures. People who are growing up and grow-
> ing old today differ from their predecessors in the markedly increased
> length of their lives, as well as in many other ways. Lives have been
> changing, but our society's compensatory structural changes lag far
> behind, producing strains both on individuals and society as a whole.
>
> (Riley and Riley 1986:51)

Structural lag is a critical concept for our exploration of the placement
decisions of the families discussed in this book. When we address the reasons for their placement decisions, it is essential to consider the issue of the
availability or unavailability of alternatives to institutionalization. Participants in this study had attempted to provide care for their relatives so that
they would not need to move into a nursing home, and for most, placing
their relative in a nursing home was very difficult. Some families based
their decision on their inability to find alternative solutions such as adequate home care or accessible housing. They generally preferred to maintain older relatives in the family and in the community. The changes in life

expectancy and women's participation in the labor force have far out-stripped the development of structural changes to accommodate families' needs in the face of such shifts. The experiences of these families need to be analyzed from the perspective of structural lag (see chapter 4).

THE PARADIGM

Riley's "aging and society paradigm" is illustrated in figure 1.1 (Riley 1994b:441). Key aspects of this paradigm include its portrayal of a di-achronic view, a multidimensional view linking past, present, and future and linking the two dynamisms of changes in lives and changes in struc-tures. It incorporates a synchronic view, a cross-sectional "snapshot," a "slice" of age strata. The perpendicular lines identify structures such as fam-ilies as they exist at different times throughout history. People and roles are interdependent, yet distinct, and focusing upon this, Riley has developed the principle of cohort differences: "Because of the effect of changing struc-tures on lives, members of different cohorts grow older in different ways." She adds: "This principle led to another interpretive fallacy: erroneously as-suming that members of all cohorts will age in exactly the same fashion as members of our own cohort . . . the *fallacy of cohort-centrism*'" (Riley 1994:436, 448, 440).

The paradigm includes cohorts, people born within the same time peri-od, and identifies the flow of cohorts through changing social institutions, such as the family. Over time, changes, such as increased life expectancy, occur in society at the level of social structure; this results in changes in so-cial institutions, such as the family, educational systems, religious institu-tions, social service systems, and work organizations. This, in turn, affects the lives of individuals while they are aging, influencing their experiences in areas such as caregiving and their own need for care. We can study the ex-periences of cohorts in different time periods in order to understand how people are influenced by structural changes, including changes in life ex-pectancy, as they age.

Riley's paradigm provides a framework for understanding the reciprocal and lifelong relationship between allocation of roles to people of different ages and socialization for roles expected to be performed at different ages (Riley 1994). This helps us to understand changes in the behavior of indi-viduals belonging to different cohorts and the relationship between social changes such as increased life expectancy and women's employment and

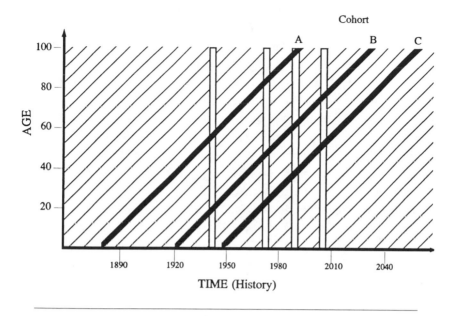

Figure 1.1

changes in the caregiving behavior of individuals within their families. The time line across the bottom of the diagram illustrates that roles within families are not fixed for all time and facilitates our ability to view changes in the care of older adults in families from a historical perspective. With Riley's diachronic, historical view of changing lives and structural change informing our theoretical perspective, we can more clearly understand the dynamics that result in changes in the care of older people by their families over time.

In figure 1.1, we can visualize the family as represented by the four sets of perpendicular lines. These are cross-sectional "slices," or "snapshots," which include members of all cohorts whose members are alive at a specified time on the time line. If we chose to do so, we could identify "slices" at all points on the time line. Riley has provided us with examples. Within any and all of the "slices," we may consider all aspects of the lives of individuals within the cohorts, focusing upon their experiences, actions, attitudes, emotions, relationships. The cohorts are represented by the diagonal lines.

This diagram can serve as a tool in conceptualizing the relationship between social changes and the circumstances of the lives of family members of all cohorts involved in making decisions about the care of family members at the present time. The current circumstances, influenced by social changes, are different from those of 1975 or 1940 or any other period of time.

The experiences of Acacia Nursing Home residents and their relatives and friends described throughout this book provide examples of caregiving at a specific time and place for a cohort of diverse individuals. Riley's paradigm helps us to understand that because structural and institutional changes occur over time, the experiences of middle-aged women in the Dominican Republic or Puerto Rico providing care for older relatives in 1900 or 1940 were likely different from those of a Puerto Rican or a Dominican woman providing care in New York City in 1995. The paradigm requires us to explore the reasons for and the implications of these changes. Likewise, there would be differences in caregiving by African American middle-aged family members in Alabama in 1935 and caregiving in an African American family in New York City in 1997 in which the mother was living at Acacia Nursing Home. The circumstances of caregiving of a Russian Jewish immigrant family on the Lower East Side of Manhattan in 1920 were different from those of a third-generation Jewish son in the Bronx interviewed for this study in 1996.

In Riley's synchronic view, it is accepted that there are changes over time in the allocation of people at particular ages to roles available to them and in the socialization of new "recruits," members of society, to meet role expectations for responsibilities such as care of older relatives.

The stories of Acacia Nursing Home residents and their relatives and friends demonstrate that people undergoing such changes as a family's initial experience with nursing home placement may find the adjustment extremely difficult. Sometimes the difficulties accompanying changes in role behavior are increased by factors that cause additional stress, as was true for Latino participants in the study who had been socialized according to the cultural expectations of another culture, as well as a different time. Sensitivity is required from social workers and others who are involved with families in helping them to understand and respond to the changes.

Riley's paradigm is valuable for formal and informal service providers, academicians, and researchers because it offers an approach to understanding the relationship between social changes over time and cohort differences in behavior. Using this paradigm as a conceptual tool, social workers and other service providers can develop a better understanding of the interper-

sonal dynamics within client systems and can arrive at appropriate interventions for empowering older adults and their caregivers.

SOCIAL CHANGE AND THE STUDY PARTICIPANTS

When the families whose relatives eventually entered Acacia Nursing Home
were confronted with the need for extensive care for a family member,
their experiences were influenced by the widespread social changes affecting the structure of families in the United States. For the majority, placing
a relative in a nursing home deviated from the caregiving decisions made by
members of earlier cohorts within their families. In 54 of the families, the
resident had no relatives who had been admitted previously to a nursing
home. This group included the families of 14 African American and Afro-
Caribbean residents, 12 Jewish residents, and 18 Latina/o residents. Seventeen of the residents—7 African American and Afro-Caribbean residents,
6 Jewish residents, and 4 Latina/o residents—had only one relative who
had previously lived in a nursing home. The effects of social changes, socioeconomic factors, or the lack of other options for acceptable care resulted in circumstances that necessitated a search for new ways to meet caregiving responsibilities that had traditionally been assumed by relatives. A
cohort change in fulfilling caregiving roles in these families occurred when
the older adult moved to a nursing home. As members of these cohorts
were confronted with new challenges and limited options, some of the caregiving responsibilities were fulfilled through nursing home placement.

The effects of contemporary social changes were reflected in information
secured from chart reviews and shared by participants during their interviews. This group of residents and their familial caregivers belong to cohorts whose average lifespan has been extended substantially. The ages of
the residents at admission ranged from 58 to 99, with an average age of 80
in each of the three ethnic groups. Likewise, many of the caregivers have
reached old age themselves: the ages of African American and Afro-
Caribbean caregivers ranged from 22 to 88; those of Jewish caregivers,
from 28 to 91; and those of Latina/o caregivers, from 25 to 72.

The most prevalent primary diagnoses at admission were cerebrovascular accidents, or strokes, which was a diagnosis for 22 (29 percent) of these
residents, and diagnoses involving cognitive loss, for 19 (25 percent). The
latter diagnoses included dementia, organic mental syndrome, cognitive
impairment related to brain hypoperfusion, and confusion subsequent to a

fall. Only 2 people had a primary diagnosis of both a CVA and dementia or diminishing cognition, and so a total of 39 (52 percent) of these residents had at least a CVA or dementia as a primary diagnosis. The effects on the residents and their relatives can be devastating, as indicated by a woman whose grandmother was rearing her at the time of her stroke:

> My grandmother had a stroke and was in the hospital a couple of months. They moved her from the I.C.U. and said O.K., this is how she is, she's paralyzed. She won't be able to do this, that, or the other things. The hospital isn't geared to do the things she needs; it's not a nursing home, so, I guess my aunt went on a search to find a nursing home.

For 27 people, 36 percent of the sample, the most prevalent secondary diagnoses were related to cognitive loss. Nineteen, or 25 percent, had a secondary diagnosis of hypertension, including 11 African American and Afro-Caribbean residents, 44 percent of the sample of African American and Afro-Caribbean residents in the study. The high prevalence of hypertension within this group of residents is consistent with epidemiological findings of high rates of hypertension within the black population in the United States (Wykle and Kaskel 1994).

Individuals may continue to live for years after developing such conditions, and many need extensive assistance until the end of their lives. Immediate death results from one in three strokes, but two-thirds of the individuals who suffer a stroke survive, and one in three strokes causes permanent disability (Moody 2002).

Addressing the diagnosis of dementia, Moody (2002:10) describes this disease as an organic mental disorder in which people progressively lose their capacity to think and remember; the disorder is "characterized by confusion and memory impairment and may manifest itself in a wide range of symptoms, such as wandering or losing things." The most common cause of irreversible dementia in old age is Alzheimer's disease, which results from the deterioration of brain cells caused by plaques and tangles; it appears to be one of the most common diseases of late adulthood (Moody 2002). Typically its victims progress through successive stages of mental deterioration until they ultimately experience serious confusion, become unable to handle dressing, bathing, and other activities of daily living (ADLs), and may become incontinent and unable to walk or speak. Shenk (2001:21) has described plaques and tangles as "cellular debris," "clumpy brown spherical *plaques* floating between the neurons, and long black stringy *tangles* choking neurons from inside their cell membranes."

The widespread social changes examined in this chapter affected the ability of many relatives to provide care at home when older family members experienced severe health problems. Fifty (67 percent) of all caregivers who were interviewed were employed outside of the home at the time of the interview, and 14 (19 percent) indicated that they were retired. One woman had recently been laid off from her job after many years of employment. Thirty-nine (65 percent) of the 60 female caregivers were employed at the time of their interview, while 11 (73 percent) of the 15 male caregivers were employed at the time of their interview and the other 4 were retired.

Changes in family structure were also evident among the residents and their caregivers. Fifteen (20 percent) of the 75 caregivers were divorced (8), separated (5), or divorced and remarried (2). Eight of the residents, 4 males and 4 females, were divorced or separated at the time of placement, and 2 other female residents had divorced and remarried early in their lives. Nine (12 percent) of the caregivers were widowed, and one was an unmarried individual living with a partner. Seventeen (23 percent) were single, and 33 (44 percent) were married at the time of their interview. Eight of the married participants were married to the nursing home resident for whom they were a caregiver; 6 were wives whose husbands were in the home, and 2 were husbands whose wife was a resident. One female caregiver was divorced from the man for whom she was the primary caregiver.

Factors related to migration and settlement in an urban area also affected the ability of families to meet traditional caregiving expectations. For some, living in apartment buildings without elevators presented accessibility challenges for people who had difficulty with mobility, and adequacy of space was also a problem for some families who would have liked for their older relative to live with them. Housing is generally expensive in this city, and accessible housing that is spacious enough to comfortably accommodate relatives is unaffordable for many people. Migration from outside of the continental United States can result in a loss of housing options that provide more flexibility, as well as loss of the potential for assistance from other members of one's family (Drachman 1992).

Riley suggests that "cohort differences in lives not only reflect the social changes of the past, they also call for present and future interventions to improve these lives" (Riley 1994a:1216). Formal and informal service providers and researchers must be able to recognize the effects of structural lag in the inability of social institutions to meet the needs of older people, and they must develop means of addressing the discrepancy between the needs of individuals in a changing society and the resources that are available.

Many contemporary circumstances affected the lives of the residents of Acacia Nursing Home and their families in ways that created barriers to their ability to perform caregiving roles in traditional ways, despite the desire of many to do so. The emotional and practical ramifications of these issues will be explored throughout this book. Members of this society have a collective responsibility to empower older people and their families to maximize their abilities to meet the challenges of reaching old age in a changing society. The problems experienced by individuals and their families at this time of life need to be understood and addressed as public issues. If we fail to accomplish that, structural lag will continue to exist.

2

RESEARCH STUDIES ABOUT
CAREGIVING BY FAMILY AND FRIENDS

She always made sure that we had enough to eat before we went to bed and so now one of us feeds her every evening to make sure that she has enough to eat before she goes to bed. —A resident's daughter, nine years after her mother's admission

THIS CHAPTER WILL REVIEW research findings from studies about caregiving that are relevant to the experiences of the 75 residents of Acacia Nursing Home and their families who are the subjects of this study. Considerable research has focused on the relationship of the caregiver to the person receiving assistance, gender and caregiving, caregiving tasks, motivation for caregiving, and emotional responses to caregiving. This chapter also includes research in the less frequently studied areas of caregiving and ethnicity and race and nursing home placement. It is notable that in many caregiving studies the racial/ethnic background of the older adults and their caregivers is not indicated and that caregiving studies have generally not addressed the significance of extended kin and fictive kin, people who may be unrelated by blood or marriage.

TASKS PERFORMED BY CAREGIVING RELATIVES

In the study at Acacia, the caregivers who were interviewed were adult children and grandchildren, husbands and wives, a former wife, friends, nieces and nephews, a daughter-in-law, and siblings of the residents. The fact that they were assisting a relative is consistent with research findings documenting that the primary providers of instrumental and emotional support for disabled and dependent older adults are relatives and friends (Mui, Choi, and Monk 1998; Shanas 1979). Research indicates that older people remain in close contact with their relatives, friends, and neighbors (Kovar 1986), and most will turn to relatives and friends when they need help (Feder, Komisar, and Niefeld 2000). In fact, since more people in the United States are living to advanced ages, family caregiving for older relatives has become more common than in the past (Toseland and Smith 1991).

Although many of the instrumental activities of daily living for the residents in the study at Acacia Nursing Home had been carried out by formal service providers since placement occurred, many of the relatives and friends who were interviewed had provided emotional support and assistance with various tasks before placement and continued to perform that kind of assistance after placement. The Acacia study and others (Dwyer et al. 1992; Seltzer and Li 2000) confirm that caregiving includes transitions involving role changes and can be reconceptualized as having some features of a career.

Although a substantial body of research exists on caregiving provided by families for older adults who are not living in nursing homes, relatively few studies have addressed caregiving issues after nursing home placement. The limited information available regarding relationships of adult children with their parents in nursing homes indicates that ties between adult children and their parents remain strong after nursing home placement, and most children who assist their parents before placement continue to provide care. While the activities may change, the person who was the principal caregiver before placement usually continues in that role (Brody 1990).

Bumagin and Hirn (2001:105) have discussed the role of family caregivers in easing the transition of relatives into a nursing home by providing "continuing empathic understanding and help." They note that caregivers can help residents to express feelings (including anger), encourage reminiscence, help the resident to recall his or her strengths and abilities, and reaffirm their relationship and interest in the resident. Brody (1990) wrote that tasks performed after placement include serving as the contact person in emergencies, visiting, grooming, bringing items such as food, straightening drawers, doing laundry, managing money, and consulting with staff about care and needs.

Many relatives of Acacia residents included in this study provided the kind of emotional support described by Bumagin and Hirn. Tasks performed by relatives and friends were also consistent with Brody's findings, since they included both emotional support and activities related to the caregiver's formal responsibilities as sponsor. Among these activities were serving as the primary contact for consultation with the interdisciplinary staff and informal monitoring of the care their relative received, as well as activities of a more personal nature, such as visiting, bringing food, translating, and shopping.

Acacia residents in the study had received assistance from family and/or friends before placement unless the debilitating conditions that resulted in placement had a sudden onset. That was the case primarily for the residents who had entered the nursing home following a cerebrovascular accident (CVA). Most of the research on task performance has looked at assistance to older people who are living outside of nursing homes and receive help with the standard set of instrumental activities of daily living (IADLs) and the set referred to as activities of daily living (ADLs). IADLs include household chores, home repairs/maintenance, gardening/lawn care, running errands, and transportation; ADLs are personal care activities, including dressing, bathing, eating, and toileting (Harootyan and Vorek 1994). The 1982 Long-Term Care Survey of the Health Care Financing Administration also classified caregiving in terms of personal tasks, including hygiene and mobility, administration of medication, household tasks, shopping and transportation, and handling of financial matters (Abel 1991; Stone, Cafferata, and Sangl 1987), and several researchers have utilized these data in their analyses of caregiving (Mui 1992, 1995; Mui, Choi, and Monk 1998; Stone, Cafferata, and Sangl 1987).

A large database that identified the relationships of relatives to older family members whom they were assisting was the Informal Caregivers Survey (ICS) of the 1982 National Long-Term Care Survey. Data were collected by the U.S. Bureau of the Census for the Department of Health and Human Services from 1,924 caregivers, of whom 72 percent were women, including adult daughters (29 percent of all of the caregivers) and wives (23 percent of all of the caregivers). Husbands were 13 percent of the caregivers and, with an average age of 73, they were the oldest of the caregivers. They spent the most extra hours in caregiving, and about half of them had no informal or paid assistance. The average age of the caregivers in this study was 57.3 years, with 35 percent 65 and over. The length of time that they had been providing care ranged from less than 1 year to 43 years, with 18 percent providing care for less than 1 year, 43.9 percent for 1 to 4 years, 20.2 percent for 5 years or more, and 16 percent no longer providing care. About 16 percent of the primary caregivers were working and 73.2 percent were not, while 49.4 percent of the secondary caregivers were working and 42.5 percent were not. Less than 10 percent of the caregivers indicated that they used paid services. Seventy-five percent of the caregivers and care recipients lived in the same household. In two other studies, however, the proportion of older people and their caregivers in shared living arrangements was lower—57 percent among caregivers surveyed in the National Long-Term Care Channeling Demonstration, 1982–1984 (57 percent) and 54 percent in a survey in eastern Massachusetts (Stone, Cafferata, and Sangl 1987).

In the study at Acacia Nursing Home, variations existed among caregivers in many aspects of their relationships with the residents. The typology of family relations developed by Silverstein, Lawton, and Bengtson (1994) is useful in understanding these variations. The data were obtained in the 1990 AARP Intergenerational Linkages Survey. The typology is based on the characteristics of geographic distance, frequency of contact, emotional closeness, consensus of opinion, giving help, and receiving help. These components of intergenerational solidarity are reduced to the underlying factors of opportunity, closeness, and helping behavior.

In order to better understand variations in the relationships of caregivers and residents in the Acacia study, it is useful to extend Silverstein, Lawton, and Bengtson's (1994) typology of ten types of child-parent relations to include not only those between parents and adult children but also residents' relationships with other relatives and with friends. From the total of ten relationship types described by Silverstein, Lawton, and Bengtson (1994:47–48), relationships of caregivers and residents in the study at Acacia are described accurately by the following six types, which reflect broad variations:

> *Tight-knit-helping*: high on opportunity, high on closeness, high on helping behavior. In this type of relationship parents and children are engaged on all three dimensions of intergenerational solidarity. . . .
>
> *Ritualized-helping*: high on opportunity, low on closeness, high on helping behavior. Contact and support persist in spite of a lack of closeness. . . .
>
> *Alienated-helping*: low on opportunity, low on closeness, high on helping behavior. In this type of relationship only helping behavior is high. We might assume that functional assistance is provided or received on the basis of a sense of obligation to the other generation. . . .
>
> *Ritualized-independent*: high on opportunity, low on closeness, low on helping behavior. In this type of relationship, opportunity for interaction is not accompanied by feelings of intimacy or patterns of assistance. . . .
>
> *Dispersed-independent*: low on opportunity, high on closeness, low on helping behavior. This type of relationship is emotionally intimate but maintained at a distance. . . .
>
> *Alienated-independent*: low on opportunity, low on closeness, low on helping behavior.

Silverstein, Lawton, and Bengtson point out that these divisions are based on the arbitrary criterion that the category is higher or lower than the average score on each dimension and so the labels for each type are relative.

MOTIVATION FOR CAREGIVING

The following is a brief overview of theoretical perspectives and research findings from the literature addressing motivating factors in family caregiving of older adults. With few exceptions, discussion of informal caregiving for older adults has focused on assistance provided by relatives to older adults who are not in nursing homes, as opposed to care provided to nursing home residents and that provided by caregivers outside of a narrowly defined family structure.

Filial piety, or filial responsibility, was a motivator for many caregivers in the Acacia study, especially Latina/o caregivers (see chapter 7). Consistent with filial piety, some of the Latina/o caregivers spoke about helping their relative because of responsibility or duty. Motivation to provide assistance to older relatives has often been attributed to filial obligation (Connell and Gibson 1997; Finley, Roberts, and Banahan 1988), with filial responsibility based on the philosophical beliefs of parental reverence, debt of gratitude, and/or friendship and love for parents (Selig, Tomlinson, and Hickey 1991). Research indicates that in the United States a stronger or more unqualified sense of filial obligation may exist among members of certain ethnic groups, including people belonging to Hispanic, Chinese, and other Asian cultures (Selig, Tomlinson, and Hickey 1991). In her discussion of Latino families, Garcia-Preto (1996:151) states: "Perhaps the most significant value they share is the importance placed on family unity, welfare, and honor. The emphasis is on the group rather than on the individual. There is a deep sense of family commitment, obligation, and responsibility. The family guarantees protection and caretaking for life as long as the person stays within the system."

Caregiving has also been attributed to reciprocity and appreciation (Abel 1991), as well as altruism (Midlarsky 1994). Another relevant concept, mutuality, is included by Jordan and her colleagues in self-in-relation theory (Jordan 1997; Jordan et al. 1991), and mutuality appeared to be particularly relevant to African American daughters in the Acacia study. This perspective emphasizes the importance of relationships between mothers and daughters throughout their lives and suggests that daughters, as well as their mothers, learn to take care of their relationship and that both attend to each other's well-being and development (Surrey 1991). Turner (1997) has addressed cultural variations within the self-in-relation model, suggesting that the possibilities for connectedness for women of color may be increased within their cultures and with members of other minority cultures. She attributes this to experiences of racial oppression and of being bicultural in the United States.

As occurs in societies, all of the caregivers in the study had been socialized regarding role expectations for care of older relatives in their cultures of origin. A theoretical perspective that increases our understanding of the development of caregiving expectations is convoy theory, proposed by Antonucci and Akiyama (1991). They suggest the idea of convoys of social support that develop over the life course and can include intergenerational relationships that reflect the importance of individual, family, and cohort developmental experiences. In describing the concept of convoy, they explain: "The basic idea is to view social relations and social support as a lifetime, ongoing set of relations that develop and change over time. These relations generally serve to enrich, fortify and reassure people but can sometimes place individuals at risk or make them more vulnerable as they move through life from birth to death" (1991:106). One component of this perspective is the idea of bidirectional exchanges and expectations between children and their parents that "exist over time and are part of a life-time of support relations which the individual maintains as part of his or her convoy of social support" (1991:105).

The findings in the Acacia study reinforce the idea of the existence of convoys of support, but vast differences existed in the size of the residents' informal support systems, confirming the reality of vast differences in the development of convoys. In the Acacia study, the informal support system of one woman included only one friend. In contrast, another resident had an extremely large family of more than 150 people, several generations of whom were involved in providing instrumental and emotional care.

Individuals' availability to provide assistance to relatives is an important issue in the performance of tasks. While some families appear to have a large convoy of many potential caregivers for older relatives, we know that certain relatives become much more involved in caregiving than others do. Within the very large family mentioned above, the granddaughter who was interviewed identified herself as the "family caregiver." She explained that she held this position because she had never worked outside her home. Of course, it is possible that she had never worked outside her home because of her decision to be the "family caregiver" for relatives, young and old, in need of assistance.

Research suggests that in spite of increased rates of female employment outside the home, the supply of informal caregivers has not been severely limited, for other people in the informal network seem to provide more assistance when the female primary caregiver is employed (Doty, Jackson, and Crown 1998). These authors present evidence that there continues to be a female "ethic of care," since the employed female primary caregivers in their study provided an average of eighteen hours of care per week. They also point out that almost half of the primary informal caregivers for older people are 65 or older themselves, and so for many people no conflict exists between employment and care of older relatives. In the Acacia study, the age range of the caregivers who were interviewed was 21 to 91. Other studies indicate that caregiving spouses, particularly wives, report unmet needs and that older adults caring for spouses with Alzheimer's disease may receive less assistance from formal and nonkin sources than other people caring for spouses (Straw, O'Bryant, and Meddaugh 1991).

Marital status appears to be a characteristic related to differences in the implementation of caregiving roles. In one study, Braus (1994) found that single women spent more time providing assistance to aged parents than single men or married people did; however, single men were more likely to provide assistance by living with older parents in the parents' home. Burnley's (1992) study of the lifestyle adjustments and emotional supports of sixteen never married women who had been primary caregivers found that while they were caregiving they had changed their lifestyles, given up activities, and limited their relationships of emotional support; some had also experienced related conflicts at work, but they were generally not angry or resentful about their sacrifices. Burnley suggested that the limitations that the women experienced were considered by themselves and others to be less crucial than the limitations that married siblings would have experienced.

Likewise, marital status of the older person in need of assistance appears to have implications for the range of caregivers who are available. Many of the residents in the Acacia study received assistance from people other than adult children or partners. In a study that compared assistance given by relatives to older people who had two or more surviving children and to those who had one or no children, Cicirelli (1981) found that the latter had stronger relationships with cousins, nieces, and nephews, although not with siblings, and received more services from kin other than children. They also wanted services from nonfamily providers more than was the case for people with two or more children, and they used more services provided by friends, neighbors, volunteer agencies, and hired service providers. They did not, however, more often turn to government agencies for services.

Barrett and Lynch (1999), using data from the 1982 National Long-Term Care Survey in their analysis of variations in caregiving networks of elderly people by marital status, found that size and composition of helping networks of married older adults differed significantly from networks of older adults in almost all unmarried groups. An exception occurred in networks of people who had been separated or divorced since their networks did not differ significantly in size from networks of people who were married. The networks of married and separated/divorced older adults were the smallest networks and included primarily relatives, and people who were married were least likely to have assistance provided by formal helpers. The unmarried older adults had more-diverse caring networks than people who were married, and the likelihood of help from friends increased as the number of children decreased. Another study (Johnson and Catalano 1981) distinguished between the experiences of married and unmarried older people without children. Married older people generally received necessary help from their spouses, while unmarried older people received assistance from siblings, nieces, and nephews. Johnson and Catalano suggested that the unmarried individuals had used a strategy of anticipatory socialization, which resulted in development of relatives and friends as resources, whereas the married individuals had employed a strategy of withdrawal from other social relationships and movement into the interdependence of marriage.

EMOTIONAL RESPONSES TO CAREGIVING

Many of the participants in the Acacia study described stressors and stress reactions to caregiving. The stressful nature of caregiving is well documented in the literature (Brody 1985; Hughes et al. 1999; Mui 1992; Rose-Rego, Strauss, and Smyth 1998; Strawbridge et al. 1997).

Research indicates that caregiving women experience more stress than caregiving men (Cantor 1983; Johnson 1983); the additional stress has been attributed to the fact that women provide more help and more hands-on help (Brody 1990). Caregiving women have been reported to experience greater role strain (Fredriksen 1996; Ingersoll-Dayton, Starrels, and Dowler 1996; Young and Kahana 1989). Caregiving wives have reported more negative psychological states compared to caregiving husbands, and this difference has been attributed to wives' greater attentiveness to their emotions and greater likelihood of reporting negative effects, wives' use of more emotion-focused coping strategies, and performance by females of more personal care and household chores (Rose-Rego, Strauss, and Smyth 1998). Other research suggests that caregiving men may experience considerable stress but may minimize it (Kaye 1997). Kramer and Lambert (1999) found evidence of reduced psychological well-being among a relatively healthy sample of caregiving husbands, who were less happy and more depressed than non-caregiving husbands in the study.

Yee and Schulz (2000) reviewed thirty empirical research reports on the effects of caregiving on psychiatric morbidity of family caregivers, published from 1985 through 1998, and they concluded that caregivers reported higher levels of depressive symptoms, clinical depression, and anxiety than people who were not providing care for an older relative. They were particularly interested in determining whether greater psychiatric morbidity (illness) exists among female caregivers than among male caregivers. The majority of nine studies that focused on gender and depression did find higher levels of depressive symptomatology in women than in men. Yee and Schulz also noted that research by Fitting et al. (1986) and Parks and Pilusik (1991) found that women had higher anxiety scores than men, and Fitting and colleagues found that female caregivers reported more paranoia than men. Studies by Chang and White-Means (1991), Collins and Jones (1997), and Rose-Rego, Strauss, and Smyth (1998) found that female caregivers reported lower life satisfaction than male caregivers. Most studies have not identified the differential effects of caregiving on psychiatric symptomatology over time, but Schulz and Williamson (1991) found in a longitudinal study that at Time 1 women reported more depressive symptoms than men, but over a two-year period women's scores remained high and men's increased to a level equal to those of women. Yee and Schulz (2000:155) note that women generally have a tendency to report higher depression levels than men but that the excess psychiatric morbidity among female caregivers does appear to be related at least partially to the caregiving experience, as indicated by "the larger difference between depression scores of women caregivers and comparable noncaregiving female community samples when compared with the difference in depression scores of men caregivers and comparable noncaregiving male community samples." They recommended that additional research be conducted pertaining to gender differences in psychiatric morbidity among caregivers, since most of the studies have focused on spousal caregivers of Alzheimer's patients and little is known about psychiatric symptomatology of other caregivers, and few of the studies on this subject have involved multivariate analysis; therefore the effects of factors such as socioeconomic status and the caregiver's physical health have usually not been considered.

Studies of caregiving suggest that the strains on the caregiver are much greater when the older person lives with the caregiver (Brody 1990). As noted previously, research has indicated that caregiving single sons are more likely than caregiving single daughters to live in their parent's home. In a study of eight daughters caring for their mothers, daughters who coresided with their mothers expressed more conflict, but caregiving and conflict strengthened attachment for some (Pohl, Boyd, and Given 1997). Peters-Davis, Moss, and Pruchno (1999) found in their study of 252 coresident daughters and daughters-in-law and their husbands that caregiving experiences were overwhelmingly more similar than different. Peters-Davis and colleagues (1999:72) suggested that issues of selectivity may arise in that daughters-in-law with closer relationships with their mothers-in-law may be more likely to choose to live with the mothers-in-law and that living together possibly "washes out the differences between daughters and DILs so that the household situations appear very similar." Hughes and colleagues (1999) found in their study of caregiving provided to veterans that coresidence was associated with greater objective burden.

Adult daughter caregivers have been reported to experience decreased levels of willingness and increased strain when they perceive no alternative to care (Berg-Weger and Rubio 1995), and daughters have experienced less stress as caregivers when the mother-daughter relationship is more peerlike at the time of the caregiving experience (Walter 1991). Abel (1991) identified specific patterns in the relationships of daughters with their mothers that were related to reviving and reconstructing relationships, responding to demands for care, and establishing limits. For women who were experiencing intimate contact with their mothers for the first time since adolescence, earlier issues unexpectedly reemerged, sometimes accompanied with intense feelings that in some cases included resentment. The experience of providing care for their mothers engendered fears of aging and death, reflection on the changes in their own lives, feelings of loss, and redefinition of their roles in relation to their mothers. Most of these women considered the need to exert authority over their parents to be difficult and believed that their mothers resented their exercise of authority.

The National Long-Term Care Survey data indicated that there is low use of formal care by family caregivers (Stone, Cafferata, and Sangl 1987). The idea that "formal care is viewed to be a last resort when the responsibilities become too complex to handle alone or with informal assistance" (Stone, Cafferata, and Sangl 1987:625) has also been supported by other research findings (Horowitz 1985a; Soldo and Manton 1985). In the study at Acacia, however, almost half (36) of the residents had received formal services just prior to hospitalization before placement or placement itself, and nursing home placement was the last resort when responsibilities became too complex for the caregiver.

Relatives experience many emotions after placement; some of the strains experienced before placement continue, while others are different (Brody 1990). Some of the participants in the Acacia study reported continued strains, but for others stress appeared to be greatly reduced after the resident and caregivers adjusted to the placement. According to Brody (1990:243),

> families of nursing home residents attribute some of their strains to what they perceive as poor care of the parent in the nursing home, negative staff attitudes towards the elderly person and the family, the physical environment, the presence of other deteriorated patients, reluctance to "complain" about care of staff because they fear retaliation on the helpless parent, and ambiguity about their own roles vis-a-vis staff. When the older person is on Medicaid, their families often fear that the nursing home will not continue to keep them because the reimbursement rate is low.

The caregivers who were interviewed in the Acacia study were satisfied with the care provided by the nursing home, most did not consider the staff's attitudes to be negative, and they were satisfied with the physical environment. In fact, their positive impression of the physical environment was a contributing factor for many in selection of this specific nursing home. They did not discuss concerns about the presence of other deteriorated patients, nor did they express concerns about their relative's being allowed to remain in the home. Some did indicate concern about ambiguity in their roles and about expressing their concerns to staff. As a staff member who was knowledgeable about roles and responsibilities of the interdisciplinary staff, the residents, and the families and friends of residents, I was able to assist in clarifying some of these issues and provide participants with the names of appropriate members of the staff for follow-up.

Research has indicated that guilt, cost, quality of care, and getting other relatives to visit the nursing home resident are important issues and that children who believe that their parents are having more difficulty adjusting report that they are having more difficulty themselves in coping with their parents' placement (Townsend, Deimling, and Noelker 1988). All of these emotional issues were brought up by some of the participants in the Acacia study. In another study, relatives of depressed residents in senior housing and nursing homes were more likely to be depressed than relatives of residents who were not depressed (Brody, Hoffman, and Winter 1987). Most of the participants in the Acacia study described themselves as depressed at the time of their relative's placement but said they were no longer depressed about placement by the time of their interview.

GENDER, ETHNICITY, AND CAREGIVING

Many of the studies of assistance provided by relatives to older adults have focused upon gender as a significant variable in the caregiving experience, but far fewer studies have addressed the salience of race and ethnicity to caregiving expectations and practices, especially for nursing home residents.

The Acacia study included sixty female caregivers and fifteen male caregivers. In this respect it was parallel to most of the research in this area, which has consistently indicated that women are more likely to be caregivers. Data from national surveys, including a study sponsored by the National Alliance for Caregiving and the American Association of Retired Persons (1997), show that approximately 70–75 percent of caregivers are women (Yee and Schulz 2000).

Seven sons and twenty-nine daughters were interviewed in the Acacia study. A substantial body of research has focused upon sons and daughters as caregivers, far more of it concentrating upon daughters. In addition to the previously reported findings related to stress and morbidity, studies indicate that female caregivers, particularly daughters, provide a substantial amount of the assistance to older relatives living outside of nursing homes, and many researchers have written that daughters are more likely to provide assistance than sons (Abel 1991; Hagestad 2000; Harootyan and Vorek 1994; Mui 1995; Stone, Cafferata, and Sangl 1987; Toseland and Smith 1991). Yee and Schulz (2000:156) cite several researchers who have argued that "women caregivers may be at greater risk for negative mental health effects because they provide more caregiving assistance in general and are more likely to help with more hands-on, day-to-day caregiving activities, such as meal preparation, cleaning, cooking, and personal care" (Horowitz 1985b; Miller and Cafasso 1992; Montgomery 1992; Stoller 1990). Research has indicated that daughters also continue to assume a larger share of responsibilities after nursing home placement (Brody, Pruchno, and Dempsey 1989).

Differences in the caregiving tasks performed by males and females have also been documented, with daughters more likely than sons to do chores that keep them constantly on call (Archbold 1983). Some studies have found that daughters are less likely to set limits and are more likely to assume responsibility for improving the general quality of life of older relatives (Abel 1991; George and Gwyther 1986; Miller 1990; Robinson and Thurnher 1979; Zarit, Todd, and Zarit 1986). Studies indicate also that daughters are more likely than sons to assume responsibility for personal care tasks (Abel 1991; Chang and White-Means 1991; Collins and Jones 1997; Kramer and Kipnis 1995) and that tasks assumed by daughters and sons tend to reflect roles that are considered gender-appropriate in the United States (Brody 1990). However, a small number of studies have not found gender differences in provision of these tasks (Fredriksen 1996; Neal, Ingersoll-Dayton, and Starrels 1997; Stoller 1990; Young and Kahana 1989). Daughters have been described as more likely to provide direct hands-on care and sons more likely to assume responsibilities such as money management and home repairs and to be involved often in major decisions (Brody 1990).

Some studies have identified other patterns in caregiving by males and females. No differences in household caregiving tasks were reported in research by Tennstedt, Crawford, and McKinlay (1993). Findings from the National Long-Term Care Survey indicated a reverse pattern in the responsibilities assumed by sons and daughters compared to that generally found in studies, and the difference has been attributed to the way the questions in that study were phrased. Responses indicated that wives were more likely to help with financial management and husbands more likely to help with household chores and shopping (Stone, Cafferata, and Sangl 1987). It is important to note that Yee and Schulz's findings from their review of thirty studies indicated that "most studies demonstrated that women spent more time on caregiving than men; however, inconsistent results were found in terms of the number of caregiving tasks performed" (2000:157).

The findings regarding men as caregivers are more compelling, and that research is relevant to this study, since fifteen of the caregivers interviewed at Acacia were male. It is well documented that many men in the United States are providing assistance to older relatives (Cantor 1983; Chang and White-Means 1991; Mui 1995; Stone, Cafferata, and Sangl 1987). Kaye (1997) has challenged the traditional approach in gerontology in the characterization of men as caregivers, suggesting that older men are heavily engaged in caregiving and that their caregiving involves significant physical, emotional, and time commitments. According to Kaye, "In the research that reports on spousal caregiving, men are generally found to provide equal or greater proportions of care, compared to their female counterparts.

Thus, marital status and age appear to play important parts in determining caring responsibility" (1997:232).

Kaye suggested that while men may minimize their stress related to caregiving, they experience a heavy burden when providing care over extended periods of time for a relative who is ill. He described male caregivers as follows:

> Men engaged as primary caregivers are, more likely than not, older husbands caring for their incapacitated wives. Indeed, it is conceivable that men constitute more than half of spousal caregivers (Archer and MacLean 1993). The majority of such individuals are likely to be in their 50s or older. The proportion of male caregivers that are men of color or representative of minority groups is difficult to ascertain, given that the vast majority of surveys of male caregiving have failed to tap the experiences of ethnic and racial minorities. While primary spousal caregivers are more likely than not to be retired, a substantial minority (perhaps around 25 percent) combine the responsibilities of caregiving simultaneously with the demands of part-time and full-time employment. The majority of primary male caregivers live with the person to whom they are providing care and, more likely than not, have resided with that person for an extended period of time.
>
> (1997:235–236)

Kramer and Lambert's (1999:665) research identified a life course transition among older husbands when they became caregivers in which they experienced "significant changes in their household tasks, social integration, marital relationships, and well-being, albeit not always in the expected directions."

Male caregivers may receive only very limited assistance from the formal service system (Motenko 1988), and research findings indicate that the perception among male caregivers that formal services are needed increases as the health of the person for whom they are providing care deteriorates (Kaye and Applegate 1990). Furthermore, when Kaye and Applegate compared the perceptions of caregiving husbands and nonspousal male caregivers, they found that husbands "believe there to be significantly lower levels of need for agency assistance than do their nonspousal counterparts" (Kaye 1997:239). Caregiving husbands may be at greater risk than wives who are caregivers, particularly those who are spouses living with the person for whom they are providing care. Kaye (1997:241) notes: "Whether motivated by male stoicism, a desire to retain control, or the gratification realized from sustaining a meaningful relationship, primary male caregivers can be observed to go it alone with minimal help received from others. Nor do they appear inclined, necessarily, to escape or flee from the responsibilities of family care." These spouses are at risk for emotional and physical health problems (Kaye 1997).

In her analysis of perceived emotional strain of caregiving sons and daughters interviewed in the National Long-Term Care Channeling Demonstration, 1982–1984, Mui (1995) suggested that sons experience less emotional strain than daughters but that no gender difference was evident when other variables were controlled. The most important predictors of emotional strain for sons were parental behavioral problems and few informal helpers, while the most important predictors for daughters were interference with work and the quality of the relationship with the parent. Noting that survey research on sons has addressed primarily "gender task differences between sons and daughters," Harris (1998:342) focused specifically on the experiences of thirty caregiving sons and identified common themes in the content of their narratives. The shared themes were duty, acceptance, taking charge, shared emotions, and work flexibility, and common issues were loss, sibling relationships, role reversal, coping strategies, and positive outcomes. Harris was also able to generate a typology of caregiving sons, which included "the dutiful son," "the son who goes the extra mile," "the strategic planner," and "the son who shares the care."

Harris suggested that demographic and social trends, including the increase in the population of older adults, smaller average family sizes, greater sibling mobility, and changing gender roles, make it probable that more sons will become caregivers for their parents. In discussion of her findings, Harris wrote: "Sons in this study were committed to caring for their ill parents and were motivated out of a sense of love and/or obligation that did not depend upon the availability of a sister. These sons were the ones providing the care, and they oriented to their caregiving roles in different ways. The role of most of the sons' wives was to support them emotionally." Services that the sons needed were information, care management, support, and respite.

Harris's research, findings in the Acacia study, and research by Delgado and Tennstedt (1997) all indicate that caregiving by Latino males needs more attention. Delgado and Tennstedt suggest that the involvement of Puerto Rican sons as caregivers should be examined because of changes in demands on Puerto Rican women that may limit their availability as caregivers, the likelihood of an increase in the size of the Puerto Rican elderly population, and the lack of previous research that addresses this issue. In their study of 106 Puerto Rican sons and daughters who were primary caregivers for their parents, the 17 caregiving sons were younger than the daughters and less likely to be married, they were more likely to live with the relative they were assisting or alone, more than half were not working, and the majority were born in Puerto Rico. Most reported Spanish as their commonly used language, although most had lived on the mainland for more than ten years.

The sons were more likely than the daughters to attribute their primary motivation for providing care to filial responsibility; they used fewer formal services, and used them less frequently than the daughters did; and they provided a wide range of assistance, as did daughters. Because the sons used far fewer formal services, the authors suggest that the demands and stress of caregiving might have been greater for sons than for daughters. The findings of Delgado and Tennstedt (1998:128–129) are contrary to traditional gender role expectations because sons provided more help with housekeeping and shopping, in addition to financial management and transportation. Consistent with gender expectations, daughters were more likely to provide personal care.

While relatively few studies have focused on ethnicity and caregiving, the available research has documented racial and ethnic differences in the size and composition of caregiving networks of family and friends (Mui, Choi, and Monk 1998). Black families appear to select caregivers from a more varied pool of helpers (Gibson 1982) and may be more likely than white families to increase the amount of help when a relative's health and functional status change (Miller and McFall 1991). Studies have also indicated that black elderly are more likely to have larger informal caregiving networks (Miller and McFall 1991; Thornton, White-Means, and Choi 1993) and are more likely than white elderly to receive assistance from relatives outside of the immediate family (Thornton, White-Means, and Choi 1993). While other kin and nonkin substitutions are made in the absence of children, adult children perform integral roles in the support system of black older adults and also play an important role in linking their parents to church support networks (Chatters and Taylor 1993:72). Black caregivers have expressed lower levels of burden (Connell and Gibson 1997; Hughes et al. 1999), and white caregivers have been found to exhibit greater depression than black caregivers (Haley et al. 1995).

Cantor (1979) found that the children of Latino older people provided more interaction and support than the children of older people who were black or white. Lubben and Becerra (1987) found that Mexican Americans were three times as likely as whites to live with a child and more likely than whites to receive help from their children with ADLs. In the Acacia study, more of the Latino residents than African American, Afro-Caribbean, or Jewish residents were living with an adult child before placement.

Results of the Acacia study indicate that caregiving experiences in the African American and Afro-Caribbean, Jewish, and Latino families varied greatly within each group. Some families in each group deviated from the usual patterns reported by researchers for their particular racial or ethnic group.

ETHNICITY AND NURSING HOME PLACEMENT

Research regarding ethnicity and nursing home placement is extremely limited. The emphasis in many of the existing studies has been on communication needs and ethnically sensitive care (Espino 1993; Espino et al. 1988; Jones and Jones 1986; Rempusheski 1989; Saldov 1992; Saldov and Chow 1994; Trilla 1982; Yeo 1993). Espino's writings (Espino et al. 1988; Espino 1993) include research results and discussion about the medical problems of Hispanic nursing home residents, describing a greater degree of physical and functional impairment at younger ages than in the white population. Yeo (1993) provides a comprehensive review of research pertaining to admission and adjustment to nursing homes, and she relates relevant research findings to specific nursing homes. The collection of essays edited by Barresi and Stull (1993) constitutes a valuable addition to the literature regarding ethnicity and long-term care. Angel and Hogan (1994) call for a research agenda that focuses upon developing a greater understanding of the diversity of the older adult population.

It has been documented that members of Latino nationalities have less experience with nursing home placement than many other populations (Espino 1993; Greene and Ondrich 1990; Hazuda and Espino 1997; Lacayo 1993; Mui and Burnette 1994). Espino and his colleagues (1988) suggest that the pervasive sense of alienation of Hispanics from the norms of the dominant non-Hispanic white population may result in the use of nursing homes only when intensive informal support efforts have failed. According to Trilla (1982:90), consideration of nursing home placement "is an even more difficult problem for members of ethnic groups such as Puerto Ricans, whose shared concepts of the extended family and duty to care for others are deeply ingrained. To compound the problem, the Puerto Rican family is faced with a lack of extended care facilities which resemble the home environment."

Notwithstanding the fact that the oldest black nursing home in the United States, the Stephen Smith Home, was founded in 1864 (Pollard 1987), black elderly are far less likely than white elderly to be admitted to nursing homes, even though they experience more functional impairment from chronic illnesses (Moody 2002). Stoller and Gibson (1994) suggest that this may occur because of caregiving patterns within black families, discrimination in long-term care facilities, or the crossover phenomenon of greater life expectancy for black elderly after they reach their late seventies (Stoller and Gibson 1994). Coke and Twaite (1995) attribute older blacks' underutilization of health care services in general to institutional discrimination.

While none of the caregivers of African American and Afro-Caribbean residents in this study indicated that the resident or they had experienced racial discrimination at Acacia, it is important to understand the history of Black older adults with regard to nursing homes in the United States in terms of the history of racism in this country. While segregation does not exist at Acacia Nursing Home, research has documented the existence of institutionalized segregation in some nursing homes. Wallace (1990) found that the proportion of African Americans in a facility was correlated with the proportion of African Americans living in the same neighborhood as the facility. Wallace advances both a cultural theory and a racial theory as explanations. The cultural theory proposes that families place elderly relatives in facilities close to their homes so that it is easier to visit, and the racial theory suggests that African Americans are steered away from white nursing homes by the professional referral network—more specifically, by hospital discharge planners—and also that African Americans avoid facilities in white neighborhoods with racist reputations.

While nursing home placement is more prevalent among non-Hispanic white elderly than among black and Latino elderly (Darnay 1998), informal care constitutes the bulk of care for white older people (Hayes, Kalish, and Guttmann 1986). Among some white ethnic groups, such as Italian Americans, nursing home placement carries a great deal of stigma because "community sanctions operate along with strong filial values to make placement in a nursing home one of the most undesirable alternatives. A child does not abandon the parent to an alternative viewed as worse than death" (Johnson 1985). For the Jewish families in the Acacia study, placement had not been the preferred option when family members believed that other options, such as home care, would meet the needs of the future resident adequately. When consideration of nursing home placement occurred, however, options for placement at an institution such as Acacia, which incorporates Jewish cultural and religious values and traditions, were available. This nursing home, founded in the mid-1800s, is part of the very broad system of Jewish social services supported by cultural values and expectations of providing care for others within the Jewish community. The fact that Acacia was a Jewish home was significant to many of the caregivers for Jewish residents, as well as to the residents themselves.

An earlier work of Dobrof (1977) focused on theoretical and practical issues in the maintenance of family ties of long-term care residents, and her work continues to be salient for issues regarding ethnicity, family, and nursing home care more than twenty years later. Dobrof suggested that while an older person may interpret placement in a nursing home as rejection by his or her children, in some families the placement occurs because the family wants the best care and living situation for their relative. This was evident in the situations of many of the Acacia residents and their relatives. Dobrof also suggested that older people who initially experience placement as rejection often feel less rejected when they see that they are not being abandoned by the family.

According to Dobrof, important issues for nursing home staff as they begin work with families of residents are an understanding of the particularities of the crisis that precipitated placement; understanding the resources, in terms of economics and people; treatment of the family as a unit of which the resident is one member; interdepartmental communication, which may be systematized in a large institution and less formal in a small nursing home; and consistent, explicitly communicated, articulation through relationship and activity of staff of the partnership between family and the nursing home. This approach helps to ensure that even though the nursing home has primary responsibility for medical and paramedical services, families will understand that they still have responsibilities. Information from the participants in the Acacia study confirms the importance of these actions.

Dobrof stated that "institutional policies, procedures, provisions, and staff attitudes affect the ability of the family to share in the care of their aged members. And second, families and the aged residents feel better if family activities are encouraged by institutions and staff" (1977:40). She described several areas in which policies and provisions in nursing homes present obstacles or facilitate participation of relatives in the lives of the residents: visiting policies and provisions for practices such as bringing food, the facilities themselves, and excursions and visits outside of the institution. Restrictions in hours and days when there can be visitors, exclusion of children as visitors, and information given to families in formal institutional language can impede family participation.

An issue that is relevant to Dobrof's observations and that is specifically related to the experiences of African American and Afro-Caribbean older adults in nursing homes is raised by Morrison's (1979) observation in her study of five nursing homes in New York City that ethnic nursing homes serving a majority of black residents were more likely to include cultural components in routine activities than nonethnic (non-black) nursing homes. At Acacia, the therapeutic recreation department has made an effort to provide more inclusive programming, planning such events as gospel music programs, available to all residents and their relatives and friends.

Dobrof devoted considerable attention to the issue of families bringing food to residents, noting that administrators of both long- and short-term institutions have considered issues related to food to be persistent problems. In several nursing homes, she observed a "cultural and ethnic" pattern of families providing food treats, such as relatives' bringing special foods for residents who were Jewish, Italian, British West Indian, Irish, and black. In the Acacia study, Latina relatives brought foods such as rice and beans.

Turning to the issue of facilities, Dobrof discussed public spaces, such as parking areas, lounges, and coffee shops, that may facilitate or inhibit family participation, suggesting that lounge areas and coffee shops open to relatives and friends are welcoming and provide both a symbolic and a real purpose. In the Acacia study, one of the features that appealed to some of the caregivers when they were choosing a home was the large outdoor garden, an area frequented by residents with their visitors. Dobrof also noted the importance of policies that facilitate residents' visits to their relatives' homes but said that institutional red tape and limitations related to federal and state reimbursement regulations were impediments for some families in the study.

The literature is consistent with the findings in the Acacia Nursing Home study indicating that extensive assistance is provided to older people by informal service providers within their kinship and friendship systems and that the tasks, motivating factors, and composition of caregiving networks of family and friends are extremely varied. While it is essential to understand individuals in terms of the intersecting variables in their lives, the literature indicates that there tend to be intragroup and intergroup similarities and differences in services, motives, and emotions that are associated with gender, race, and ethnicity as aspects of culture.

Caregiving is generally stressful for females and males, although caregiving males may be less likely to show outward manifestations of their stress. Support systems vary in size and participation, and although socialization into convoys of support occurs, the kinship support systems of caregivers in the study at Acacia Nursing Home ranged from a support system of one person for one resident to more than 150 people of many generations for another. Members of some groups who are less accustomed to caregiving, such as Puerto Rican sons, may find themselves increasingly in this role because of the effects of demographic changes and may lack adequate support because they are assuming culturally nontraditional roles.

The significance of race and ethnicity in placement planning and experiences of families is reflected on the micro, mezzo, and macro levels in the limited literature on ethnicity, race, and nursing home placement, as well as in the research at Acacia Nursing Home. Variations in attitudes and experiences with nursing home placement are related to cultural expectations within racial and ethnic groups, as well as mezzo-level expectations of families and friends. For example, Dobrof noted the significance for some residents and their relatives of the provision of ethnic food. On a macro level, the literature suggests that social attitudes in the United States have resulted in racially discriminatory practices by some hospital discharge planners. Notwithstanding the pervasive racism in this country, caregiving relatives and friends of African American and Afro-Caribbean residents in the Acacia study did not believe that race affected Acacia Nursing Home's provision of services to their relatives.

3

EARLIER YEARS: LIFE WITHIN
FAMILIES AND COMMUNITIES

My mother used to do everything for everybody. Everything that they needed they asked for. —A resident's daughter, ten months after her mother's admission

She had some money friends, fair weather friends who were there only when she paid them for something. —A resident's friend, one year after her friend's admission

Whenever there was a hole, the family asked her to fill it up. . . . She was the spokesperson for her mother. She took her everywhere.

A resident's niece, seven years after her aunt's admission

THIS CHAPTER IS ABOUT the earlier adult lives of the Acacia residents, their lives before they developed the conditions that resulted in nursing home placement. It is about their relationships with relatives, friends, and other acquaintances in their communities. They knew neighbors in their apartment buildings; participated in religious organizations; developed relationships with coworkers; and were active in political organizations, voluntary organizations such as the Girl Scouts, and self-help organizations, including Alcoholics Anonymous.

Life within their families was an important aspect of their earlier experiences, and the family relationships of some residents in each group were influenced by their migration or immigration experiences. Sometimes their moves involved separation from relatives and friends permanently or temporarily. In this chapter, *migration* refers to movement within national borders, and *immigration* refers to movement across international borders. The movement of African American residents from the South to the North in the United States, of an Afro-Caribbean resident from St. Croix in the U.S. Virgin Islands to the U.S. mainland, and of Puerto Rican residents from the island to the mainland is referred to as migration. The movement of Afro-Caribbean residents from Anguilla and from Jamaica, that of Jewish residents from England, Germany, Poland, and Russia, and that of Latina/o residents from Cuba, the Dominican Republic, Ecuador, and Mexico is referred to as immigration. Drachman and Ryan's stage-of-migration framework, with its stages of premigration and departure, transit, and resettlement, is a useful concept for understanding residents' earlier immigration and migration experiences and subsequent moves into the nursing home (Drachman and Ryan 1991; Drachman 1992).

FAMILY RELATIONSHIPS

It was pretty much my grandmother and I. . . . Our little family net consisted of my grandmother, my mother, my aunt, her two kids, and myself. That was really our close knit family so, of course, contact was daily between all of us. Other family members which she may have had spread out. You'd hear from them once a month, once a year, you know, but it was really the six of us.
    —A resident's granddaughter, eight years after her grandmother's admission

Family relationships were important in the Acacia residents' earlier lives, and many had maintained close contact with relatives over the years. Although disruptions in family relationships had occurred for some residents who immigrated or migrated, as for residents who had relatives who moved to other geographic areas, most of the residents had at least one relative living in the city where Acacia was located. For many, cultural expectations appear to have reinforced maintenance of family contacts. An African American resident's cousin noted that her own mother had reared the resident in the South and that in her family the expectation was that they would maintain contact with relatives.

In each group many residents and families had maintained close intergenerational ties throughout their lives. An African American resident who had lived with her daughter for three years before going into the nursing home had been visited daily by her children, grandchildren, and greatgrandchildren. Her daughter described her as always having taken care of other people—her seven children and other people's children. A Jamaican resident who had been separated from her husband for thirty-five years and lived alone was visited and helped financially by her daughter, who described her as a helper; she gave money to her neighbor even if she was destitute herself, and she gave to others through her volunteer work in a hospital and in the housing project in which she lived.

Many of the residents had lived alone for years but were an integral part of their families and communities. For example, an African American resident who lived by herself was described by her daughter as receiving frequent visits from her son, grandchildren, sisters, neighbors, and members of her church, as well as almost daily visits from her daughter at the end of the workday. An African American resident who was a widow saw her two daughters frequently; one visited every other day and the other visited once a week, and her granddaughter and great-grandchildren also came to see her. In addition, she remained in contact with her sister in Alabama by telephone. One of the Jewish residents was a woman who had developed a chronic illness at an early age, and this resulted in the need for assistance from her daughters. However, she also helped her daughter on an ongoing basis and was a source of advice and support for her friends. For one of the Puerto Rican women, the primary role in relation to her adult children was to provide support. She was in contact with them frequently, visiting three or four times each week with her daughters who lived locally and talking on the telephone weekly with her daughter who lived out of state. Her nephew was a daily visitor.

Some of the residents had lived with relatives throughout their entire lives, while others had done so intermittently. A son said that his mother continued to live in the house in the Dominican Republic in which she had grown up, and her daughter and her family lived with her. In 1976, she visited her sons in New York City, then remained there and made it her primary residence. She continued to alternate between living with her sons in New York City and in the Dominican Republic. In both countries, she was also visited frequently by her children with whom she was not living. Another son said that his father, from Puerto Rico, had lived with his sons intermittently after his separation from his wife in 1980, and the amount of time spent living with them had become more frequent for a few years before admission to the nursing home. He was described as primarily taking care of himself but as being supportive of his children, helping them financially and talking with them if they were depressed.

Residents living with younger relatives were integral participants in their families. One resident had lived with her daughter and her family since her immigration from Ecuador in 1966, and her daughter and granddaughter said that she had raised her three grandchildren. She took her granddaughter to school, helped with school bake sales, and participated in class trips. She cooked every Sunday for family gatherings, which included additional relatives, and she visited daily with her sister, who lived in the apartment next to hers.

Residents who lived with adult children generally maintained contact with other relatives. An Ecuadoran resident talked by telephone once each month with her sisters and brothers in Ecuador, maintained contact through letters, and in 1975 traveled back to Ecuador for a visit. An African American resident who had always lived with her daughter had grown up in a close-knit family and community. She talked with her sister daily and remained in contact by telephone with friends she grew up with in Virginia. She liked social contacts but preferred planned rather than spontaneous visits. A resident from St. Croix lived with her daughter and maintained contact with other relatives and friends by telephone every day. Her daughter described her as concerned about her daughters and her friends and "being there for them."

An African American resident had lived most recently with her daughter in New York and had previously lived with her sisters in Michigan and Georgia. She spoke on the telephone weekly with her brother, sisters, and daughter, and her nieces visited her. Her daughter described her as a kind-hearted, compassionate person who was always willing to help sick neighbors and did whatever was needed for others. An African American woman described by her niece as "a bit independent" lived with her divorced sister and her sister's children until they were grown, and then her sister moved out of their home in the early 1970s. She was very close to her two sisters and visited with them every other week, maintaining telephone contact between visits and also maintaining contact with her niece.

Sometimes relatives lived in other apartments in the same building. A Puerto Rican resident who had always lived with her mother or her brother was described by her niece as having other relatives who lived in the same apartment building. She visited almost daily with her brother and sister who lived in the building, and her nephews and nieces also visited. She had lived with her younger brother for fifteen years before moving to the nursing home, and she contributed to their household by cooking and cleaning, as well as sewing for her family until she lost her sight in one eye a few years before admission to the nursing home.

Several of the Jewish residents had lived with a sibling for all or a considerable part of their lives. One resident who lived with her sister also saw or spoke by telephone with several cousins once a week. Another resident had lived with her mother until 1964, lived alone from 1964 to 1970, and had lived with her sister since 1970. Her sister described her as having always been dependent emotionally and intellectually on her family and as relying on her sister for assistance in making decisions.

A Jewish resident who had become a widow at a young age had lived with her sister since 1963. They belonged to a small family, but they lived in the same building as her son and his family and saw them daily. In her home, she assumed responsibility for all of the housework and shopping and occasionally sewed for her son and his family, as well as sewing and cooking for neighbors and friends. Another resident's niece said that her aunt had lived with her mother for her entire life until her mother died, two years before her aunt entered Acacia Nursing Home. Her niece said that their family was influenced by European cultural traditions, and the expectation was that her aunt, as the younger daughter, would take care of her parents. During the years that her aunt was employed, her mother had assumed housekeeping responsibilities, and after her aunt retired she did the housework. She was the spokesperson for her mother and took her to doctors' appointments and anywhere else that she needed to go. She was also in contact with at least one of her two nieces daily, either in person or by telephone. This resident was the person who was described in the quotation at the beginning of this chapter as filling up any hole where help was needed in the family. According to her niece, her life was highly structured, and friendships outside the family were very limited.

Some residents lived their lives almost totally within their nuclear families rather than as part of an extended family. A wife described her husband's familial relationships as caring and reciprocal interaction with his wife, sister, son, and daughter. Family interaction was also limited for a Jewish resident who had little contact with relatives after his marriage in the 1950s.

At least one resident in each group had been married for forty years or more, and the spouse was now the caregiver. The wife of one of the Jewish residents described her husband as a person who had led his life in an active and independent manner and whose social contacts with relatives were primarily with his wife's family. A husband who had been married to his wife, one of the Jewish residents, for fifty-one years before her placement in the nursing home described her as having loving, caring relationships with relatives and others. He said that he and his wife loved and helped each other. Their other relatives lived far away and visits were infrequent, but his wife was in contact with her sisters and others at least monthly. Similarly, the wife of an African American resident to whom she had been married for fifty-six years said that they had little contact with relatives but that her husband had a lot of friends and did for others, sometimes staying with a neighbor who needed help until someone could come to be with that person. The husband of another African American resident said that his wife was a person who helped relatives and friends but that as she became older she had little contact with relatives.

One of the Jewish residents had been married to his wife for almost fifty years, and his relationships had been primarily with relatives rather than friends. He spoke on the telephone at least monthly with his sisters who lived in Florida and was in contact with his cousins and daughters. He paid the household bills, washed the dishes, and ran errands as long as he could. According to his wife, when he was no longer able to assist her "he still wanted to be able to help."

Caregivers described several of the residents as persons who tended to stay to themselves and had limited social contact with relatives. The friend of an African American resident described the resident as always living alone and not being in contact with relatives. The two had been friends for around twenty years; they would see each other because she worked in the laundromat and the resident would come in daily. This is the person described by her friend as having money friends; she said that "she didn't help other people unless they helped her and then she would pay them." A friend who was the primary caregiver for another African American resident said that her friend had lived with a family for whom she did domestic work for fifty years, and then she lived with her brother and his daughter after a few years of living alone.

Some of the Jewish residents also had limited contact with their extended family. A son described his mother as a woman who stayed to herself and got together with relatives only occasionally. She was married until her husband died in 1992, and her visits with other relatives were with her son, daughter, daughter-in-law, and brother. A daughter whose mother had been a widow for four years described her mother in a similar manner. A man whose wife had died in 1983 was described by his sister-in-law as having social contacts only with one of his sons and herself after his wife died. Generally, he had not been involved with relatives or others. A daughter-in-law described her father-in-law, who had lived alone for a year after his wife went into a nursing home, as quiet and unsociable, with contact primarily with his sons and their families. A niece described her aunt as living alone almost all her life. Visits with relatives were infrequent, since they lived in another part of the city, but her niece described her as always wanting to invite relatives to her home. She talked with her niece and her sister approximately once each week. Another niece described her uncle, who lived alone in the same place for forty years, as estranged from most of his relatives because of his alcoholism. His closest family contacts had been with his brother, who spoke with him by telephone once or twice a month, and his cousin, who visited occasionally.

Some of the Jewish residents lived far from all or some of their relatives, and this distance limited contact. The primary caregiver of one resident, her sister-in-law in a Midwestern state, said that the resident had become a widow at a very young age and had lived alone in senior citizens housing for around twenty years before going into the nursing home. This resident spoke with her sister-in-law monthly and stayed with her sister-in-law and her family when she visited them on special occasions. One resident's son lived in another part of the country, and it was because of her contact with her grandchildren in New York City that she was able to spend time with relatives. She had lived alone for a long time after her divorce, eventually remarried, and remained married until her husband died in 1991. Her grandson and granddaughter visited her once a week, and she liked to cook meals for them. She was also in contact weekly by telephone with her thirty-four cousins.

Although most of the Latina/o residents had relatives who lived in the city, many also maintained contact with relatives living elsewhere. The niece of a Dominican resident said that several of her aunt's relatives lived in Alabama and Delaware and that they had maintained contact by telephone and mail, but visits were infrequent. Her contact had been primarily with her niece, granddaughter, and daughter. Another resident had daily visits and phone contacts with relatives who lived in New York City and also maintained contact by telephone with her brother in Puerto Rico. Another Puerto Rican resident had children who had continued to live in New York City and other sons and daughters who had moved back to Puerto Rico in 1970. She spoke with her children in Puerto Rico by telephone and visited them for three or four weeks at a time. One of the other Puerto Rican residents had two daughters living in New York City and a daughter in Florida; her daughter in Florida phoned every Sunday and visited on some of the holidays.

PARENTING AND GRANDPARENTING

She did her job. She did not play. You would go to school. You would get an education. My father and she raised 9 children, 5 of their own and 4 nieces and nephews, and they all turned out well.

> —A resident's daughter, two years after her mother's admission

Their roles as parents and grandparents were important for many of the residents. Forty-one of the caregivers who were interviewed were the residents' children or grandchildren. The relationships of the residents with their children and grandchildren after they became adults varied, however, even within the same family. For example, the son of one of the Jewish residents said that his mother had not had any contact with her other son in more than twenty years, but she saw this son five or six times a week because she walked to his office almost every day to visit him.

Many grandparents who lived in the same home as their grandchildren had helped with their care. Several children and grandchildren of Puerto Rican residents described their experiences in this way. A daughter whose father had lived with her for more than twenty years said, "He was a good help with my children and with everything in the home." A granddaughter who described her grandfather as active and independent stated that his social relationships were with his family, primarily with his daughter, son, and granddaughter, and that he had helped to rear her. Describing her grandmother as a person who had taken care of her, another granddaughter said that she felt that she had experienced role reversal because she now takes care of her grandmother.

Some of the residents had continued, during much of their lifetime, to share their homes with children and grandchildren who were dependent upon them. According to one niece, her aunt always took care of her son, and she also had considerable contact with her many cousins and other relatives, some of whom lived with her at various times. One of the other residents had a son, age fifty-four, who had lived with her since he was born. This resident had also visited almost daily with her sisters and daughter, reared her granddaughter, and helped to pay for her sister's college education. She was described as helping everyone, doing for others, and listening.

Two of the African American residents had reared granddaughters who became their primary family caregiver after their admission to the nursing home. One granddaughter described her grandmother as a very independent woman who had been a widow for a long time and who "kept the family together; she was active and involved in everyone's life. She was in control of everything." She had remained in the city but had bought her daughter her house in the suburbs. Another granddaughter described her grandmother as living alone for most of her life except for an occasional roomer. She was in contact with friends and neighbors a few times a week, and every three or four months her granddaughter would call her.

INDEPENDENCE

She was a bit independent.

—A resident's niece, one year after her aunt's admission

Nursing home residents are generally thought of as dependent in many ways even though some are able to maintain their autonomy in some areas. Relatives and friends who have known them for many years, however, know that they were not always as dependent, that in reality some of these individuals were very independent. In the research interviews at Acacia Nursing Home, fifteen of the residents, particularly Latinas, were described as having been independent, and *independence* was a term used to denote self-sufficiency. Describing a person as independent did not mean that the person lacked contact with others.

One of the Puerto Rican residents was described by her brother as wanting to be alone and not complicate her life. While she was still living in Puerto Rico, however, her sister-in-law came from Arrecibo to the resident's home in Salinas to visit her daily, and neighbors also visited her. In addition to this, she was in contact with others through her employment in a hospital and her work in the institutions in which she volunteered.

The nephew of one of the Jewish residents said his aunt had lived alone for more than thirty years after her husband died in the early 1960s. He described her as independent, cautious, and conservative, living on a low income. A few times a week she visited with her nephew, sister-in-law, and friends who lived in her apartment building. Another resident was described by her sister as always having been very self-sufficient, as taking care of herself even before the death of her husband several years before her placement in the nursing home. Although the sisters talked daily on the telephone and visited often, they had not needed to assume responsibility for providing assistance to each other.

Some of the residents who were described as independent had assumed a great many responsibilities in caring for their children and, sometimes, their grandchildren. One resident had come alone to the United States from the Dominican Republic as a widow in 1951 and had brought her six children later. She worked to support her family and was still working after her grandchildren were born. Because of her employment, she could not help with care of her grandchildren, but her daughter described her as a person who did everything for everybody, "everything they needed they asked for." Her children visited her two or three times each week, and for this woman giving to others also included participation in her church.

Some of the other residents had persevered in caring for their children despite extremely difficult circumstances. In describing her mother's earlier life, a daughter said that when her mother was still living in Puerto Rico her first husband was murdered, leaving her a widow with four daughters. Two years later she married again, and subsequently five more children were born. After her children became adults, the mother continued to be in daily contact with at least one of her daughters; her daughter described her mother as independent until one year before admission to the nursing home.

A Puerto Rican man described as very independent lived by himself from the time of his separation from his wife in 1975 until he moved into his son's home three years before admission to the nursing home. He helped his son with chores such as shopping, and generally his relationships were primarily with relatives. His daughter and granddaughter lived in an apartment in the same building, and he visited with them almost daily, helping with tasks such as taking his granddaughter to school if his daughter was unable to do this. He spoke with relatives in Puerto Rico by telephone every three to four months.

Some of the residents who were described as independent liked to cook or provide housing temporarily for others. Another Puerto Rican resident had lived alone until a year and a half before moving to the nursing home, and her daughter described her as always having been a person who wanted to do as much as she could for herself, not wanting to be dependent. Her children visited her once each week, and she phoned them almost daily. She liked to cook for her children and for members of her church. An African American resident who lived alone and had daily contact with her children and grandchildren through visits and telephone conversations was described by her daughter as independent and always doing for others, helping her family and "so-called friends." Her daughter said that she fed people, gave them money, offered them showers. Another African American resident was described as always wanting to take people in, feed them, and give them a place to stay; her husband and she had reared four nieces and nephews in addition to their own children, and she had helped with her granddaughter's care.

Some residents had helped their families financially. One Puerto Rican resident was described by his granddaughter as living in a three-generation family that had included his wife and himself, their daughter, and his granddaughter. He had been like a father to his granddaughter because her own father had died when she was five, and her mother and she had lived with her grandparents while she was growing up. Her grandfather was very active and independent, and although he was always working he made himself available to his family if they were in need of money, a ride, or other sorts of help.

Other residents had provided assistance to persons outside of their families, but migration to the mainland could affect patterns of interaction. One resident who was described as active and not wanting to be restricted, even after placement in the nursing home, lived in a small town in Puerto Rico and was known to everyone in the town. Her children had moved to New York, but she continued to live in Puerto Rico and visited frequently with her brothers and sisters, nieces and nephews, and cousins who lived in the same town. She "helped everyone" and used to cook for others. Her contact with others was all face-to-face because there were no telephones in the town. She lived by herself in Puerto Rico until a car accident in 1984 in which her leg was broken; then she moved to the mainland and lived with her children until entering a nursing home. Three years later, she transferred from the first nursing home to Acacia Nursing Home. She remained very independent after moving to the mainland and did not need or want help. She did, however, experience much less freedom after her move because she would not ride on the buses or subways alone, and in Puerto Rico she had been able to walk everywhere.

PARTICIPATION IN OTHER COMMUNITIES

When she was younger, she was involved in P.T.A., Girl Scouts, that was basically her life. Even when we were too old to be Girl Scouts she stayed in, and she was a Girl Scout leader. We weren't even in scouting anymore, but that was very important to her. When we were in school, P.T.A. and stuff like that was important to her. She wasn't a person who visited and brought cakes, that wasn't her.

—A resident's daughter, two years after her mother's admission

In addition to their relationships with family and friends within and outside of ethnic communities, some of the residents had participated in formal organizations. These experiences varied within each ethnic group, but there were some similarities in organizational participation across all of the groups.

The residents' community participation had included experience in the workplace. The majority of all the female and male residents in each of the three groups had been employed outside of their home at some time in their lives. Some of the women had spent many years as single parents supporting themselves and their children, and others had shared the responsibility of supporting their family with their husband or had worked temporarily at some time in their lives.

Residents had also been involved in many voluntary organizations. The resident from St. Croix had participated in activities at a senior citizens center, but she stopped going as "her friends dwindled down." A Jewish resident had spent some of his time presenting lectures at a Jewish organization. A Puerto Rican woman was active in her political party's local organization, helping with political campaigns and assisting people with immigration, housing, and other problems. A Jewish resident volunteered on election day at the polls.

Each group included some people for whom religious beliefs and practices were important. Relatives of the Jewish residents in this study spoke the least about their relatives' participation in formal religious organizations but discussed the importance for the residents and their families of the residents' living in a Jewish nursing home.

The caregivers of many African American residents discussed the residents' history of participation in religious organizations. For some, church activities had remained important for many years. One of the residents had been a member of the same church for more than fifty years and was very active in her church; church members had remained supportive of her after her admission to the nursing home. Another resident was described as "the mother of her church," and another had been very involved in her church through an auxiliary called the Go Forth Workers, visiting sick persons through the auxiliary; she also served in the dining room and participated in the senior choir. A resident who was very active in her church in Georgia helped people when they were sick, cooking and visiting. She was also a deaconess and a Sunday school teacher.

Among Latinas, a Dominican woman was described by her daughter as a person who helped her church and helped other people through her church. Her relationship with the church had continued after admission to the nursing home, as the church was providing communion to her in the nursing home. A Puerto Rican woman was also described as helping people in her church, and the resident from Ecuador had enjoyed socializing with other church members.

IMMIGRATION AND MIGRATION

In the Dominican Republic, she lived in the house where she grew up, and her daughter and her family lived with her.
> —A resident's son, one year after his mother's admission

Cultural expectations affected the placement experiences of residents and their families in all of the ethnic groups. All of the residents had been socialized earlier in their lives regarding expectations about care of older relatives, many of them while growing up in places other than the city where Acacia is located. The formation of attitudes and expectations about intergenerational relationships and caregiving in other times and places and the actual immigration and migration are relevant to the experiences of families throughout the nursing home placement process. It is important to understand the meaning of nursing home placement within different cultural contexts.

A look at several of the primary theories developed to explain why people emigrate from countries in which they are living and immigrate to foreign nations can enhance an understanding of the significance of immigration and migration experiences in the lives of residents and their relatives in this study. After I describe these perspectives, I will discuss internal migration within the United States and review Drachman and Ryan's stage-of-migration framework. The discussion will then lead to specific applications of the immigration theories, perspectives on internal migration, and the stage-of-migration framework to the experiences of residents of Acacia Nursing Home and their relatives.

Theoretical Perspectives on Immigration

The primary theoretical perspectives on immigration are (1) the push-pull model, (2) the structural imbalancing of peripheral societies perspective, and (3) social network theory. The push-pull model proposes that factors exist to "push" persons to leave the nation in which they have been residing and to "pull" people to move to a specific other location. In differentiating the theories, Portes and Rumbaut (1996:271–272) have contrasted the push-pull model as an individualistic theory with the theory of structural imbalancing of peripheral societies and social network theory, which they identify as structural theories:

> The most common theoretical approximation to the origins of immigration is the push-pull model. It is constructed around "factors of expulsion" (economic, social, and political hardships in the sending countries) and "factors of attraction" (comparative economic and political advantages in the receiving countries). The model has a close affinity to the "cost-benefit" approach to immigration advanced by several labor economists and corresponds to the popular view that the movement occurs primarily because of the motivations and actions of the newcomers. . . .

Undeniably, individual migration is determined by calculations of advantage, but these are embedded in a context that "push-pull" or "cost-benefit" models fail to apprehend. To do so effectively, we must consider two different types of social structures: those linking sending and receiving countries and those linking communities and families in places of origin and destination.

Portes and Rumbaut (1996:272) question the assumption of the push-pull model that greater disadvantage naturally leads to greater migration: "International migration, including labor migration, often originates in countries at intermediate levels of development and, within them in urban and rural sectors possessing some economic resources. In addition, there are marked differences in propensities to migrate among countries and communities at comparable economic levels." Much of the international migration that takes place occurs when people leave countries with an intermediate level of economic development rather than a low level of development. Nevertheless, the experiences of some Acacia Nursing Home residents who had migrated or immigrated clearly illustrate the salience of "push" factors. For example, this was true for Jewish residents who belonged to families fleeing persecution in Russia in the early 1900s, but their experiences also reflected the "pull" of communities in the United States where there were other persons of Jewish ancestry who could aid in their adjustment.

The second theoretical perspective, the theory of structural imbalancing of peripheral societies, holds that there is "a close association between the history of prior contact, colonization, and influence of powerful 'core' nations in weaker or 'peripheral' lands and the onset of migratory movements out of the latter" (Portes and Rumbaut 1996:272–273). For example, the Latin American countries of Mexico, Puerto Rico, and Cuba were "each in its own time, a target of a North American expansionist pattern that remolded its internal economic and social structures to the point that would-be migrants were already pre-socialized in American ways even before starting the journey."

The process of structural imbalancing of peripheral areas of the world economy, followed by sustained immigration, has taken successive forms during the history of capitalism. Deliberate labor recruitment, such as the employer initiatives that gave rise to U.S.-bound Mexican migration, represents an intermediate form of a historical process that has ranged from coerced labor extraction (slavery) beginning in the sixteenth century to the present self-initiated labor flows. . . .

Self-initiated migrations are a product of the twentieth century, where external imbalancing of peripheral societies does not take the form of organized coercion or deliberate recruitment. Instead, mass diffusion of new consumption expectations and the electronic transmission of information about life standards in the developed world suffice to encourage emigration. The gap between modern consumption standards and the economic realities of backward countries plus increasing information about work opportunities abroad provide enough incentives to generate an almost limitless supply of would-be migrants.

(1996:274–275)

Relating this perspective to the premigration experiences of Dominican, Latin American, Puerto Rican, and West Indian residents in the study at Acacia Nursing Home, it is apparent that the residents had immigrated/migrated from places that had a history of previous contact, colonization, and the influence of powerful "core" nations such as the United States. These areas can be considered "peripheral" in terms of economic resources at this point in time. We do not know the personal effects of U.S. expansionism on residents and their relatives before their journeys to the mainland United States; as one example, though, it is well known that the impact on Puerto Ricans of contact with the mainland government since Puerto Rico was ceded to the United States by Spain in 1898 has been very significant in multiple institutional areas.

In a discussion of the third perspective, social network theory, Portes and Rumbaut address international migration as "simultaneously a network-creating and a network-dependent process":

Not only differences between countries but differences *within* countries in propensities to migration require explanation. Again, a push-pull model proves insufficient at this level since families and communities of similar socioeconomic condition can produce very different migration histories. The main alternative explanation at this level is based on the concept of social networks. Once an external event such as the presence of labor recruiters or the diffusion of information about economic opportunities abroad triggers the departure of a few pioneering immigrants, the migration process may become self-sustaining through the construction of increasingly dense social ties across space.

The return of successful migrants and the information that they bring facilitate the journey of others. To the extent that migration abroad fulfills the goals of individuals and families, the process continues to the point that it becomes normative. When this happens, going abroad ceases to be an exceptional affair and becomes "the proper thing to do," first for adult males and then for entire families. At some moment, networks across international borders acquire sufficient strength to induce migration for motives other than those that initiated the flow. People move to join families, care for children and relatives, or avail themselves of social and economic opportunities created by the ethnic community abroad.

(1996:276–278)

The applicability of the social network theory to the experiences of some of the Acacia Nursing Home residents and their relatives who were immigrants and migrants is apparent. Historically, cities in the eastern United States have been ports of entry for immigrants and migrants, and the adjustment of immigrants has been facilitated by earlier migrants who have welcomed the newcomers into ethnic communities. Communication and travel back and forth from the point of origin to the point of settlement in the mainland United States had sustained social ties for members of many immigrant and migrant groups. For example, there were Puerto Rican residents at Acacia who had moved back and forth between the mainland and Puerto Rico, including a period of residence in Puerto Rico following retirement. An important sustaining influence in the networks of some of the Puerto Rican residents was that of relatives, including children, living in each location.

Although African American residents at the nursing home participated in migration rather than immigration, their earlier life experiences support the idea of the importance of social networks in migration experiences. Migrating from the southern United States to the North, many residents had become members of kin and nonkin communities that provided support to new migrants and facilitated adjustment to northern urban life. Some of the Acacia residents and their caregivers who had migrated to the North had maintained a network of relationships with persons in southern communities. As with some of the Puerto Rican residents, the network for some African Americans at Acacia had also been sustained by relationships with their children living in each location.

Internal Migration

Migration within the United States was a life experience of many of the African American residents in the Acacia study, twenty of whom were born in southern states: Alabama, Arkansas, Georgia, Louisiana, Mississippi, North Carolina, South Carolina, and Virginia. African American migration to northern urban areas during the twentieth century has been documented in historical and sociological studies and in the life stories of many African Americans.

Three distinct, but interrelated, conceptual orientations in black urban history identify historical processes that are relevant to the experiences of the African American residents in the study at Acacia Nursing Home: (1) the race relations model, which was the prevailing model from the beginning of the 1900s through the 1950s; (2) the ghetto model, popular from the early 1960s through the 1970s; and (3) the proletarian model, building upon the ghetto model and analyzing African American migration as a historical process (Trotter 1991).

According to Trotter (1991:1), "The race relations model elaborated the socioeconomic push-pull explanation of black population movement, and analyzed black migration as a pivotal element in changing race relations"; this approach, primarily sociological and social anthropological, included urban community studies, special case studies, and general syntheses of existing knowledge, with a secondary theme of African American migration as a historical phenomenon. The ghetto model analyzed African American migration as a process of historical change and applied the push-pull concept to explain African American migration, analyzing the impact of push-pull factors on the development of largely segregated African American housing and community life in cities. The proletarian approach also analyzed African American migration as a historical process, but it examined the impact of migration on the development of social class formation and paid particular attention to the development of the urban industrial working class. However, Trotter has suggested that some writers employing this approach have given inadequate attention to the influence of the southern African American experience, including African American kin and friendship networks, on African American migration.

The reasons for northern migration of African American residents in the Acacia study were not disclosed unless they pertained to declining health in later adulthood that precipitated the decision to move closer to children living in the North. It is essential for service providers and researchers to understand, however, that critical life experiences of many older African Americans are consistent with the conceptual orientations of African American urban history described by Trotter, and these experiences influence the viewpoints and realities of later adulthood. Socioeconomic push-pull factors have influenced the northward movement of many African Americans from the South who are in the same cohorts as the residents, and it is definitely the case that socioeconomic realities have reflected the prejudice and discrimination that have manifested themselves in the inequalities and deprivation suffered by a great many older African Americans in the United States. It is also likely that African American residents would have lived at some time in largely segregated urban housing and communities, consistent with the ghetto model of black urban history. The focus of the proletarian approach on social class formation is also relevant to experiences of the cohorts of the Acacia residents, particularly the emphasis on development of the urban industrial working class. Realities pertaining to social class have a powerful influence on the experiences of many African American older adults. It is also important, however, to note that some of the writers who have employed the proletarian approach have given inadequate attention to the influence of African American kin and friendship networks and therefore have missed a vital aspect of the lives of African Americans at Acacia Nursing Home and of other African Americans who provide and receive substantial assistance from relatives and friends.

The Stage-of-Migration Framework

The stage-of-migration framework developed by Drachman and Ryan (Drachman and Ryan 1991; Drachman 1992) is a useful approach for analysis of the experiences of the Acacia residents in this study. Intended to assist social workers in understanding the experiences of persons who are immigrants to the United States, the framework will be used here with regard to Acacia residents who have migrated to the United States and within the United States. This framework facilitates the development of a more thorough understanding from the perspective of the individual's unique historical experiences related to his or her ethnic heritage, the effects of migration experiences on the kinship system, and the expectations of nursing home residents and their relatives regarding care of older relatives.

Drachman and Ryan's stage-of-migration framework describes a process of premigration and departure, transit, and resettlement, including specific variables that Drachman and Ryan consider to be critical at each stage of the migration process. In this view, which sees immigration as a recurring phenomenon, Drachman (1992) posits that the framework can be applied broadly to immigrant groups in general and also can be used to assess the individual within the context of his/her experiences.

Consistent with Matilda White Riley's contextual view of the effects of social change on cohorts, which was described in chapter 1, the stage-of-migration framework views the individual as a person who functions within the context of different environments at different times and the environments as themselves being subject to change. The stages and their critical variables are presented in table 3.1.

In the stage-of-migration framework, critical variables are identified in the experiences of immigrants and refugees during the premigration and departure, transit, and resettlement stages. During the first stage, individuals may make difficult decisions and experience interpersonal losses within the context of social, political, and economic systems. Sometimes their experiences are violent and life-threatening. The transit stage includes the journey, arrival, and relocation process, and the loss of significant others. Resettlement is influenced by the degree of cumulative stress throughout the migration process and involves cultural issues and opportunity structures, as well as the reception from the host country and the discrepancy between expectations and reality.

Drachman (1992) has pointed out that the framework assumes that migration is a recurring phenomenon, that all immigrants have an experiential past, and that the model can be applied to all immigrant groups, specific groups, and to the individual. There were many variations in the experiences of the residents and their caregivers in the Acacia study, which is consistent with Drachman's point that the migration experience is not the same for all persons (1992:68). When the framework is applied to the Acacia residents in this study and their relatives, the factors that are relevant vary for individuals of different ethnic backgrounds. For the six Jewish residents who were born in Germany, Poland, and Russia, separation from family and friends, life-threatening circumstances, experiences of violence, and loss of significant others were realities for their families, as well as decisions regarding who was to leave and who would be left behind and the act of leaving a familiar environment.

As Portes and Rumbaut (1996:101) have noted, "not all immigrants were sojourners. . . . Jews leaving the Pale of Settlement and czarist oppression literally 'burned their bridges behind them.'" Elaborating upon this, Portes and Rumbaut (1996:105) say: "The movement was neither free nor temporary because most of those who escaped the czarist autocracy never intended to return. This was especially the case for the two million Jews who left Russia between 1890 and 1914." Four of the Jewish residents at Acacia had immigrated as children from Poland, Russia, and Canada

TABLE 3.1   STAGE-OF-MIGRATION FRAMEWORK

Stage of Migration	Critical Variables
Premigration and Departure	Social, political, and economic factors
	Separation from family and friends
	Decisions regarding who leaves and who is left behind
	Act of leaving a familiar environment
	Life-threatening circumstances
	Experiences of violence
	Loss of significant others
Transit	Perilous or safe journey of short or long duration
	Refugee camp or detention center stay of short or long duration
	Act of awaiting a foreign country's decision regarding final relocation
	Immediate and final relocation or long wait before final relocation
	Loss of significant others
Resettlement	Cultural issues
	Reception from host country
	Opportunity structure of host country
	Discrepancy between expectations and reality
	Degree of cumulative stress throughout migration process

Source: Drachman 1992:69.

(born in England in 1910) between 1913 and 1921. The two Jewish residents who immigrated to this country in the 1940s were from Poland and Germany and lost relatives in the Holocaust.

For the Latino and West Indian residents in this study, social factors related to migration from Puerto Rico and St. Croix and immigration from Anguilla, Cuba, Dominican Republic, Ecuador, Jamaica, and Mexico were significant. While their migration often resulted in separation from family and friends and involved the act of leaving a familiar environment, life-threatening circumstances and violence do not appear to have preceded their departure. Of course, there are other immigrants from Latin America and the Caribbean who have left their countries in order to survive such circumstances.

Twenty-two African American residents were born in the United States, and most had lived in the city where Acacia is located for many years. Their migration also involved decisions about who would leave, separation from family and friends, and the act of leaving a familiar environment. Twenty of the African American residents had migrated from the segregated South, where violence resulting from racism was directed at African Americans. Lemann (1991:14) has written: "In the late 1880s Mississippi and the other Southern states, emboldened by Washington's post-Reconstruction hands-off attitude toward the South, began to pass the 'Jim Crow' laws that officially made blacks second-class citizens. The Mississippi constitution of 1890, which effectively made it impossible for blacks to vote, was a model for the rest of the South. After its passage, the new political order of legal segregation was fully in place." Beckett and Dungee-Anderson (1992:280) have noted that "many of the current elderly blacks grew up in the rural, agricultural South where they had few rights and privileges. Laws as well as customs prevented them from actively participating in and receiving rewards from the larger society."

Consistent with Drachman and Ryan's stage of premigration and departure, a shared experience for several of the African American, Afro-Caribbean, Jewish, and Latino residents was that in the experience of their move to this city they had made the decision to leave some or all of their relatives and friends and to move far from significant others and from their familiar environment. However, network theory suggests that some of the residents had a network of relatives who also moved or they had relatives or friends already living in this city. Hraba (1994) has also noted that departure from a familiar environment and separation from family and friends are difficult aspects of migration to a distant place, and resettlement in an ethnic community can provide a source of support during and after the transition.

Although many of the residents were not recent migrants or immigrants, in this city they had been able to remain closely connected with their ethnic cultures through participation in their families and interaction with other persons who shared their heritage. Participation in ethnic communities was particularly apparent for sixteen of the Latino residents and one of the Jewish residents who had a limited knowledge of English. Drachman and Ryan (1991) suggest that foreign-born elderly persons with limited language skills can experience increased isolation.

Drachman and Ryan (1991:623) also reported that "the heterogeneity of American society acts as a social support for newcomers, as many are able to find members of their group residing in the immigrant communities in the United States. These communities provide informal assistance, which is observable in neighborhoods where the spoken and written language of the groups and the habits of the cultures are expressed." According to Portes and Rumbaut (1996:54), "for members of the immigrant generation, spatial concentration has several positive consequences: preservation of a valued life-style, regulation of the pace of acculturation, greater social control over the young, and access to community networks for both moral and economic support." Seventeen of the residents had lived in the neighborhood in which the nursing home is located and in which there is a large Latino population. Throughout the twentieth century, there also have been African American, Afro-Caribbean, and Jewish communities in this city.

Hraba (1994) suggests that psychological and social functions served by communalism for members of minority groups include structure for the lives of group members and socialization into the values and traditions of the group, including standards of self-worth. He notes that communalism can provide the opportunity for people to "see themselves as whole people, competent or incompetent, good or bad, in accord with their own criteria" (551). He does suggest that communalism, while providing psychological relief from oppression, can also isolate members from outsiders. For the residents and their families, resettlement had occurred within a nation in which they had minority status due to language, religion, race, or ethnicity. An experience shared in the United States by members of all of the ethnic groups discussed in this book is their history of a problematic reception from the host country, manifested in prejudiced attitudes and discriminatory behavior on the part of that country. Drachman and Ryan (1991:624) write: "Newcomers, although physically accepted, are predisposed to a situation of social marginality." Portes and Rumbaut (1996:55) note, however, that "ethnic communities have been much less the Trojan horses portrayed by the xenophobes than effective vehicles for long-term adaptation."

The seventy-five Acacia Nursing Home residents who are included in this study experienced similarities and differences in their earlier lives in their interaction with relatives, friends, and other acquaintances in their communities. The extent of their interaction with relatives and other persons varied greatly. In many families, there had been extensive contact throughout their earlier lives, but for some residents in each group the number of persons with whom they interacted was diminished by migration, immigration, or other circumstances. Knowledge of the major theoretical perspectives regarding immigration and of Drachman and Ryan's stage-of-migration framework facilitates our understanding of the effects of premigration, departure, transit, and resettlement for the residents who had these experiences.

Broad social, economic, and political changes affected the lives of those in the residents' cohorts, but their stories also reflect diversity of experiences related to differences in the histories of their specific ethnic groups. Within each group, it is also apparent that further differentiation among the residents exists, on the basis of personal characteristics. As Drachman (1992:68) suggests in her discussion of migration experiences, "it is assumed that age; family composition; socioeconomic, educational, and cultural characteristics; occupation; rural or urban backgrounds; belief systems; and social supports interact with the migration process and influence the individual or group experience in each stage." Micro-, mezzo-, and macro-level influences shaped the individuality of each of the residents throughout his or her life and influenced interaction with family, friends, and neighbors, as well as participation in the workplace, secular voluntary organizations, and religious organizations.

Variations in the residents' personal relationships resulted from individual characteristics, values, normative expectations regarding behavior on the part of members of each ethnic group, and social changes. Some residents appeared to have limited contact with relatives and friends throughout their lives, while others had frequent contact with large numbers of relatives and/or friends over their entire lives. Some demonstrated strong preferences for interaction within their immediate nuclear family, while others preferred interaction with other relatives or persons outside the family. The relationships of some of the residents varied over the years because of immigration, migration, and other circumstances.

The significance of nursing home placement for each of the seventy-five residents and their relatives and friends must be understood within the context of their own cultures and personal histories. This approach helps us to develop an individualized understanding of each resident's placement and adjustment process.

4

CHANGING HEALTH,
CHANGING RELATIONSHIPS

I took her to the bank and to pay bills as she got older. She had a big, big heart. I'd
leave the job and take her on my lunch hour. There was no one else to do it, and I was
close at hand. I could jump in my car and be there in forty minutes. . . . It became more
and more. . . . She asked me to take care of her. It chopped off my life at a point when
I was getting a little older, when I wanted to drop a hook in the water.

—A resident's nephew, four years after his aunt's admission

A S LIFE CONTINUED for the residents and their relatives and friends, all of the residents reached a time when they needed assistance because of changes in their physical and/or cognitive functioning. This chapter focuses upon the changes in those relationships when the resident had debilitating conditions that did not result in immediate placement but in the need for assistance with instrumental activities of daily living (IADLs) and/or activities of daily living (ADLs) at home. As indicated in chapter 2, IADLs include household chores, home repairs/maintenance, gardening/lawn care, errands, and transportation, and ADLs are personal care activities, including dressing, bathing, eating, and toileting. The most prevalent diagnoses for the residents at the time that they were admitted to the nursing home were strokes (CVAs) and problems related to cognitive loss, conditions that are most likely to occur as people become older and that can result in chronically impaired functioning (see chapter 1).

The severity of debilitating health conditions and the availability of family, friends, and agency services were critical variables for the residents in their efforts to remain at home. Some experienced long-term changes in their health that affected their lives and the lives of their relatives or friends for many years before they were admitted to a nursing home, and others remained in good health until a few months before admission or until a sudden change mandated admission. Eight of the African American and Jewish residents functioned without assistance with IADLs or ADLs until almost immediately before a hospitalization that preceded admission to the nursing home. All of the Latina/o residents and forty-two of the African American and Jewish residents experienced illnesses that resulted in the need for assistance with IADLs and/or ADLs for a period of time from a few months to more than twenty-five years before placement.

Many of the residents received extensive informal assistance from relatives and/or friends, as well as services from formal home care providers, before circumstances changed to a degree that made nursing home admission necessary. Informal assistance ranged from monitoring the work of formal home care providers, to chores including shopping and housecleaning, to twenty-four-hour supervision and assistance with IADLs and ADLs for persons in need of almost total care who received no services from formal care providers. Some of the informal caregivers lived with their relative who needed assistance, and others lived in separate households. In addition to the informal care, between four and twenty-four hours of assistance from formal home health care providers was provided daily by publicly funded agencies.

Although some of the residents were able to receive in-home services and some residents and caregivers would have preferred for the resident to remain in his or her own home or the home of a family caregiver longer, sometimes, when needs for care increased, it was ultimately decided that the available home care was inadequate and placement was necessary. The alternative to publicly funded care, assistance paid for privately, is very costly, particularly when care is necessary for twelve to twenty-four hours daily, and many people cannot afford the fees. Although in-home services are available to many older adults, structural lag exists and is apparent when older adults cannot obtain adequate services outside an institution. Service providers are accustomed to working with older adults who may be "falling between the cracks" and are ineligible financially for publicly funded services that allegedly provide a "safety net." The failure of society to put in place such a safety net of home care and other services that would more adequately address the problems and needs of older adults and their families in ways that would facilitate their ability to live in the community longer is clear evidence of structural lag in a society with high life expectancy and increasingly complex demands on families.

CONDITIONS OF THE MIND: DEMENTIA, DEPRESSION, MENTAL ILLNESS, AND THE NEED FOR ASSISTANCE AT HOME

She changed completely. The worst part was that she became very violent.

—A resident's daughter, two years after her mother's admission

Forty-six (61 percent) of the residents had either a primary or secondary diagnosis related to cognitive loss at the time of their admission to the nursing home, and many had remained in their homes with assistance from relatives for several years after they began to develop these conditions. Consistent with the results of other research on caregiving and dementia, this study found that such a situation was a physically and emotionally demanding experience for many of the caregivers.

Many of the Latina/o residents experienced cognitive losses and received informal and formal assistance because of difficulties related to their changes in functioning. Shortly before the admission of one of the Latinas to a first nursing home, her family had arranged for home care services because her cognitive functioning had deteriorated and she needed supervision all the time. In 1984, after she broke her leg in a car accident in Puerto Rico, she moved to the mainland to live with her daughter and son. She had not wanted or needed help for many years, but eventually she needed assistance from informal and formal caregivers.

Most of the Latinas/os who experienced cognitive losses lived with the condition for years before they were admitted to a nursing home. For example, the cognitive functioning of a Latina who lived with her daughter for ten years before admission began to deteriorate before she moved into her daughter's home. She began to call her daughter at three and four o'clock in the morning to complain that her neighbors were noisy, and her daughter began to help with cooking and housework because her mother was no longer doing these tasks for herself. Her daughter made the decision to have her mother move to her home because her mother needed help, space was available, she was employed nearby, and the neighborhood was safe. In another family, the woman who later entered the nursing home was limited in her activities for several years because of arthritis but also began to experience memory loss, which became so severe that she would forget her son in a minute or two when he phoned from another state to speak with her. Although she received twenty-four-hour home care for a few years before nursing home admission, her daughter also provided assistance with housekeeping chores.

Several of the African American residents had also experienced cognitive losses before placement. One of the women was forgetful and had hallucinations that appeared to be related to dementia. Her granddaughter attempted to monitor her functioning, even though she lived a considerable distance away. Although this woman was resistant to home care, she received eight hours of assistance daily. Several of the other African American residents were diagnosed with Alzheimer's disease. The wife of one of the men became aware of the extent of his cognitive loss when he was unable to find his way home from the next building one day. She provided all of his care for the next three years without the assistance of formal home care services but was supported in her caregiving efforts by participation in support groups sponsored by a veterans hospital and the local chapter of the Alzheimer's and Related Disorders Association. In the case of another resident, more than seven years before she entered the nursing home, her daughters brought her to New York City from a southern state to live with them after they became aware of the extent of her impaired functioning. One of her daughters was employed, and so she took care of her on weekends and during her vacations, while her other daughter took care of her on weekdays. Another woman who lived with her daughter had Alzheimer's disease for many years before placement, and she received formal home care services eight hours a day, five days a week, but her daughters also provided a substantial amount of care. Caregiving was difficult for her daughters because she was often uncooperative and stayed awake at night.

The functioning of one of the Jewish residents had begun to deteriorate ten years before placement in the nursing home, and this became apparent to relatives when her ability to maintain her apartment deteriorated. She lived with relatives for more than three years before admission, and they monitored her functioning. A man whose former wife assisted him for many years had problems with his "mind wandering." A resident whose relatives lived in the Midwest spent less time with them as she experienced increasing memory loss and disorientation.

Several of the other Jewish residents with deteriorated cognitive functioning needed assistance for less than one year before admission. A nephew felt obligated to help his aunt when her cognitive functioning deteriorated during the nine months before her admission to the nursing home; he was designated her power of attorney, made certain that she had food, arranged and monitored home care, and established a network of emergency contacts. Another woman lived very independently until six months before she went into the nursing home, but during those six months her daughter began to notice unpaid bills and so she began calling daily, visited more frequently, and monitored her mother's safety and behavior. Although her mother was resistant, the daughter also assisted with shopping and cleaning. The son of another resident with dementia assumed responsibility for his mother's financial affairs and monitored her care for six months before her admission. She also received assistance from a home health aide for four hours a day during this time. Another resident with dementia received twenty-four-hour home care that was paid for privately, and her daughter visited and monitored the care. As time went on, her mother had less contact with some of her other relatives because they had also become older and neither she nor they could travel easily.

Several of the Jewish residents either began to develop problems with their cognitive functioning or had previously suffered cognitive losses that became apparent after the death of a person who was important to them. A woman who had lived with her mother her entire life developed confusion related to dementia after her mother's death seven years before she moved into the nursing home. Her nieces monitored her functioning and daily twenty-four-hour home care, which was provided inconsistently, until her admission. The grandson of another resident reported that the death of her sister-in-law seemed to "rattle" her. After that loss, it appeared to her grandson, who visited weekly, that she had panicked and that she began to have difficulty maintaining her diet and hygiene, as well as taking care of her apartment. The cognitive and physical functioning of another resident deteriorated between the time of her husband's death and her admission to the nursing home three years later. Her son thought that she might have experienced memory loss related to dementia before her husband's death but that it had not been apparent because his father covered for her. After his father died, he helped his mother with financial matters, giving her a monetary allowance, and assumed more and more of the responsibilities that his mother had formerly taken care of herself. He tried to give her responsibilities, but she was unable to complete the tasks adequately.

Some of the residents whose cognitive functioning remained more intact were considered by relatives to have been depressed. Some Latinas were described as depressed for several years and received assistance from relatives during that time. A resident who moved to this city from the Dominican Republic in the 1980s lived with each of her sons at different times and became depressed after some of her children married. She had been considered the "boss" of her son's home, but after she became depressed she relinquished the responsibilities that she had assumed in his home and did less for herself. Her son thought that she might have become depressed because she could not solve all of the problems of her children.

The daughter of another Latina said her mother was depressed for about fifteen years before admission to the nursing home. The daughter gave her mother substantial assistance, often helping her before and after work with laundry, shopping, and other chores. Although a brother moved in with their mother, the daughter continued to coordinate the assistance provided to her mother. In another family, a Latina who had lived with her mother all her life was described as depressed much of the time after her mother's death. Her relatives became concerned about her eating habits and began to monitor her diet.

Some among the Jewish and African American residents had also experienced prolonged periods of depression. A Jewish resident who had been very independent was described as depressed before his hospitalization and subsequent placement in the first nursing home in which he lived. Other residents were characterized as experiencing depression, sadness, or withdrawal from social activities after the loss of a specific person to whom they had felt close emotional ties. A Jewish resident whose husband had died eight years before she was admitted to the nursing home became very sad after her husband died and did not want to be alone but also did not want anyone living with her. Before his death, she had been very self-sufficient and did not need help. An African American woman who had been living with her daughter had attended a senior center, but she did not want to go there anymore "as her friends dwindled down." When she needed assistance with IADLs, her daughter helped with cleaning and shopping, explaining, "I wouldn't want to see her struggle."

Some of the residents had experienced other psychological difficulties before admission to the nursing home. An African American woman was described as having psychiatric problems for more than twenty years before placement and had periodically stopped taking her psychotropic medication. Her husband provided ongoing assistance until his death, and by that time she was also developing dementia. The daughter of another African American resident spoke of her mother as a person who "seemed to be calling out for help." Before placement, her mother had resumed drinking alcohol excessively, threw tantrums, and was frequently going to the hospital thinking that she was physically ill even if she was not. Her daughter helped as needed, visiting and assisting her financially.

DISEASES OF THE BODY: PHYSICAL ILLNESS AND THE NEED FOR ASSISTANCE AT HOME

My mother had a stroke in her sixties, and also had glaucoma, so she was legally blind early on, and so people helped her out. They would shop for her, bake a cake for her, or come to visit her.   —A resident's daughter, two years after her mother's admission

Many of the Acacia residents had experienced physical illnesses that resulted in changes in physical functioning, but they remained at home for various periods of time before nursing home admission. Some experienced physical losses at relatively young ages and had received extensive assistance for many years from their families, friends, and/or home health care providers from agencies. A Latino man who had multiple sclerosis was unable to walk for six years before admission to the nursing home, and relatives provided shopping and cooking for him, tasks that he either prevented his home attendants from doing or that they chose not to do.

Some of the residents had remained in their homes for various periods of time following one or more strokes. One man had lived with his daughter and her family for more than twenty years after moving from Puerto Rico, and he had a stroke in his early sixties but was not admitted to a nursing home until he was seventy-six. His health gradually deteriorated after his stroke, his personality changed, and he became progressively more angry. He received assistance from a home care worker for six hours a day, and his daughter provided care on the weekends and after five o'clock on weekdays and her husband and children also helped with his care. Eventually he could not be left alone at all. Another Latino's health progressively deteriorated after his stroke three years before admission to the nursing home, and his wife took care of him and their three young children. Since he needed help day and night, it was almost impossible for his wife to sleep. He did not receive home care services until two and a half months before he was admitted to the nursing home, and then he received assistance for five and a half hours a day, but he did not let the home care worker help him. His sister stayed with him a few times when his wife took their children to medical appointments, and a year before he moved to the nursing home his mother-in-law came to live with them to help with household chores. An African American man moved into his cousin's home after a stroke and was admitted to the nursing home less than a year later. His cousin said that caring for him had not created more work for her because she had been doing tasks like cooking for herself anyway.

Contact with relatives and friends living farther away became more limited for some of the Jewish residents as they developed additional medical problems. The wife of a resident explained that her husband had difficulty walking, as well as other medical problems, and because these problems interfered with traveling to visit relatives in other states they maintained contact by telephone. For another resident who could not walk, and also developed dementia, contact with her older sisters and brothers decreased because it was difficult for them and for her to travel.

In some of the African American families, the residents had lived longer than most of their relatives or had little contact with relatives outside of the immediate family because of their own and their relatives' poor health. A husband who had been married to his wife for almost fifty years had provided assistance to her for almost twenty years because of her medical problems, and as time went on they had less contact with their relatives, who were older and also in poor health.

Many of the African American residents had needed assistance from others for many years because of medical problems. A woman who was diabetic had her toes amputated twenty years before she went into the nursing home, and a friend helped her with shopping, cooking, and laundry. Another woman had a stroke thirty years before going into the nursing home, and so her daughter and some of her friends shopped for her and a neighbor brought a hot meal to her every day. Another woman had eight strokes in twenty years and also experienced seizures. She lived alone and received home care for eight hours each day, as well as receiving a very substantial amount of assistance from her relatives. Her daughters and sons, sisters, and brother-in-law each checked on her at least three times a week, and her children asked neighbors to look out for her because even when it was difficult for her to help herself she always wanted to help people by taking them into her home to give them a place to stay. The niece of another woman helped her with shopping and banking after a stroke that occurred five years before admission to the nursing home. Members of her church also visited and were supportive to her. Another woman developed glaucoma and lost most of her vision, and although she lived with her daughter she eventually needed daily twenty-four-hour care, which infringed upon her daughter's privacy. For a couple in their late eighties, the wife's assistance to her husband included taking him to the bathroom at night, but his care became progressively more difficult for her after he developed bladder and prostate problems. They received no home care services.

Likewise, some of the Jewish residents needed assistance for several years because of physical problems. One of the women continued to live in her own home for twenty-five years though she had a fall and walked with difficulty; she needed twenty-four-hour home care for three years before placement after her ability to take care of her ADLs and IADLs declined. A man who had Parkinson's disease received home care, and his son and daughter-in-law supervised his home health aides, assumed responsibility for his financial affairs, and brought food when he was not eating adequately. He did not take his medications regularly and became disoriented at times, and as he became weaker he began to dial 911 when he was distressed.

There were also residents whose living conditions contributed to their need for help from relatives when their health changed. A Latino who had a stroke in his early sixties lived in an apartment building without an elevator, and eventually he could not go out at all. A Latina who lived with her daughter and her family in an apartment on the fourth floor of a building without an elevator became more dependent upon her family for assistance after surgery in 1983, and she rarely left the building since there was no elevator. As time went on, it became more difficult for the rest of the family to leave her because of her care needs, and so her niece, who lived in the same building, occasionally stayed with her while they went out.

As indicated in chapter 3, some of the residents had been living with relatives before they developed a need for assistance because of physical or cognitive losses. Some had been helping relatives with specific tasks, especially if they lived in the same home. As their health declined, they could sometimes no longer handle these responsibilities, and other family members stepped in to help. The Latina who had been hospitalized in 1983 had been cooking for her family, and relatives began to assume that responsibility when they concluded that she should no longer cook. One of the Latinas who became depressed used to sew for her family, and when she lost her vision in one eye she was no longer able to do so. In some families relatives tried to create tasks that they believed the person with declining health could still do. The sister of a Jewish resident said, "We sort of pushed things for her to do."

Sometimes the onset of severely debilitating illnesses occurred less than a year before nursing home admission. An African American woman who had been very independent moved into her daughter's home when she needed assistance following the amputation of her leg six months before admission to the nursing home. A Latino who was characterized as very independent needed little assistance until he began experiencing tremors and falling because of Parkinson's disease. In addition to help from relatives, he received nine hours of home care daily for five months before he moved into the nursing home. A Latina who had lived on the mainland many years ago and subsequently returned to Puerto Rico had a stroke that resulted in difficulty walking and speaking. Her neighbors in Puerto Rico visited her daily and helped her with food and showers, but her relatives became uncomfortable with this arrangement because they considered the assistance to be "charity" since it was not provided by family. Relatives living on the mainland arranged for her to to live with them so that they could take care of her themselves, and she received no formal home care services.

HOME CARE SERVICES:
COLLABORATION AND CONFLICT

It is apparent that although relatives and friends provided very substantial assistance, African American, Caribbean, Jewish, and Latino residents at Acacia also received formal home health services from agencies for various periods of time before admission. Although home care workers often provided needed assistance with IADLs and ADLs, many relatives continued to help with these or other tasks and monitored the work of the home care worker.

Some of the relatives reported that they worried about the formal care provided to their relative who had needed assistance before admission or they identified specific experiences that had been problematic. The daughter of a Jewish woman who had lived alone for many years said that she always worried about her mother and that she monitored the care provided by her mother's twenty-four-hour home attendant. A Latina who lived alone received assistance from her daughter, son, and son-in-law, as well as from a home health aide, and help from her relatives included monitoring of her home care services. An African American woman lived alone and received assistance from a home attendant twenty-four hours a day because she had become forgetful and disoriented, even leaving cooking gas turned on. In spite of the home care assistance, her daughter described herself as doing "everything," which included paying the rent and visiting almost every day after work. This woman's son, sisters, and grandchildren also visited, as did members of her church, where she had been the "mother of the church."

Sometimes the provision of home care services was problematic because home care was needed but the person who needed the assistance did not want it. The Latino who was mentioned previously as having Parkinson's disease received home care services for five months before his admission but did not want his home attendant to provide much assistance. A Jewish resident who had difficulty breathing for many years after bypass surgery received home care for eight hours each day, but he did not want this assistance although he continued to receive it until he entered a nursing home.

Some of the African American relatives who were monitoring home care services described difficulties with the services. The nephew of a resident said that he had worried about his aunt constantly even though arrangements had been made for daily twenty-four-hour home care. He experienced problems with a home attendant who did not arrive and another who did not speak English. The sister of another woman who had home care twenty-four hours daily believed that one of the home attendants had been hitting her sister and that another had left her unattended. Monitoring her care became more difficult for relatives because eventually it was more difficult for her to communicate with them.

Extensive assistance for residents of all three groups was provided through informal and formal support systems and made it possible to delay institutionalization for various periods of time, until services in the community were no longer adequate to meet the care needs. Information about their experiences clearly indicates that informal caregivers provided extensive assistance to residents with deteriorated health for periods ranging from a few months to more than twenty-five years and that residents and their families in all groups also arranged for formal services to supplement informal caregiving. Some of the residents themselves had provided assistance to relatives and friends when they were younger (chapter 3), and changes in the responsibilities assumed in reciprocal family relationships became necessary as residents developed debilitating conditions and needed assistance.

The influence of early socialization regarding cultural expectations of caring for older relatives appeared to remain strong in all groups in spite of structural changes in this society that have resulted in changes in the social circumstances under which caregiving is provided. The experiences of the individuals in this study are consistent with the research findings cited earlier indicating that family members generally provide extensive assistance to older relatives who are in need of help. For these residents, even when formal services were available, at least one individual in most of the families was involved in providing assistance before nursing home placement.

Variations in the experiences of the residents and their families before nursing home placement are a reminder that in order to truly understand the experiences of individuals as they proceed through their lives it is important to view life stages from a biopsychosocial perspective that considers all relevant variables. The lives of individuals and their relatives in the years preceding placement were diverse. In addition to the experiences described in this chapter, the study included eight residents whose biopsychosocial functioning was affected less by cognitive or physical changes until a change in health that occurred shortly before admission.

5

THE PLACEMENT PROCESS:
DECISIONS AND TRANSITIONS

*We all five sisters and brothers talked and they said whatever I would do would be all
right with them. Everybody agreed except me. For me, it was a terrible thing to do.*
—A resident's daughter, nine months after her mother's admission

THIS CHAPTER BEGINS with a description of issues regarding the
health and living situations of the Acacia residents that resulted in
the decision for nursing home placement. Discussion of the decision-making process follows, including comparison of the experiences of
families in this study with those of families who participated in other studies that have addressed these same issues. Specific points explored here include the extent and nature of participation of relatives, residents, and social service and health care providers; emotional reactions of residents and
relatives; and reasons for choosing this nursing home.

The beginning of the transit stage of nursing home placement is the part
of the placement process that occurs between the premigration and departure stage and the resettlement stage. As indicated previously, the stage-of-
migration framework for nursing home placement is a theoretical approach
to understanding the process, modeled after Drachman and Ryan's stage-of-
migration approach developed to explain a process experienced by migrants
and immigrants (Drachman 1992; Drachman and Ryan 1991; Kolb 1999).

Some of the families wanted the residents to continue to live at home,
but that was not possible because of the residents' health problems and the
lack of adequate informal and formal services to meet the residents' needs.
Changes in functioning increased the need for care provided by others, and
the decision was made by relatives and/or the older adult who needed assistance that adequate care could be provided only in a nursing home setting. The placement process often occurred rapidly, was extremely difficult
emotionally, and was frequently contrary to role expectations among the
older adults and their relatives. Within some of the families, placement de-
fied cultural expectations and was experienced as a major disappointment
and betrayal.

RESIDENTS WITH PRIMARY DIAGNOSES
RELATED TO PHYSICAL FUNCTIONING

As previously stated, the most prevalent primary diagnoses at admission were cerebrovascular accidents (CVAs), which was the diagnosis for twenty-two (29 percent) of the residents in this study, and cognitive loss. Nineteen (25 percent) of the residents had the latter as the primary diagnosis, including dementia, organic mental syndrome, cognitive impairment related to brain hypoperfusion, and confusion subsequent to a fall.

Strokes precipitated the largest number, fourteen, of resident placements following a period of no more than a few months of deteriorated health, and physical problems affecting mobility were major contributors to the need for placement. Rapid onset of debilitated functioning also accompanied hip problems involving breaks or other surgeries, and colostomy surgery. When there had been surgery, the families often expected that the nursing home stay would be limited to short-term rehabilitation, after which the resident would be able to return home and receive adequate care there. However, the nursing home stay for all of the residents in this study became a long-term stay.

Sometimes residents had been able to function very self-sufficiently until a sudden stroke or strokes occurred in rapid succession, and sometimes other health problems existed but did not impede self-sufficiency. In other situations, physical functioning was already severely impaired by other medical conditions, but the resident had been able to remain at home until the stroke increased the need for assistance beyond what could be made available.

For example, the sudden onset of physical problems resulting in placement occurred for a man who had been able to function very independently until he experienced a massive stroke that resulted in extensive cognitive loss and inability to walk. Although his wife and children wanted to provide his care at home, there were situational factors that were important considerations in the family's decision to choose nursing home placement. His care needs were too great for his wife to assume without assistance, and since all of his children lived in apartment buildings without elevators, it was not feasible for him to move into any of their homes. As mentioned earlier, some of the difficulties encountered by relatives and friends as potential providers of health-related services were related to the economic constraints imposed by the expensive housing market in this city.

Many other Latinas/os experienced similar difficulties. A resident who before her stroke was able to function relatively independently and to assist relatives with tasks like cooking was given the prognosis following her stroke that she would never walk again. Although her daughter who was most involved in providing assistance wanted her mother to live with her so that she could provide the help that her mother needed, the daughter's apartment building had no elevator. She had looked for another apartment but was unable to find one that would be adequate for her mother and herself. Another daughter said that her father, who already had diabetes, needed a great deal of care after having two strokes in the same month. She could not move him into her own home because he needed so much care, and she lacked adequate space and time. She said that perhaps she could have taken care of him in her home if he had been able to do a little more for himself, such as walking and preparing himself a sandwich. Another family, deciding after their relative's stroke that her care needs were too great for her relatives to meet them adequately at home, considered nursing home placement in Puerto Rico, as well as in the city where Acacia is located. The resident had relatives in both places, and after comparing the available care and the cost, they decided that placement at Acacia would be preferable.

Some of the residents who entered the nursing home because of the effects of a stroke had experienced serious medical problems for various lengths of time before their stroke, but the stroke was the reason for increased care needs that resulted in their admission. A Jewish resident with a history of heart problems had bypass surgery and twenty-four hours later had a stroke. After receiving physical therapy at the hospital, he was admitted to the nursing home for additional therapy and needed to remain there because of his extensive care needs and because his wife had medical problems herself and could not provide adequate care for him. He was paralyzed on his right side and had severe difficulties with his speech.

In another family a son and other relatives considered several options when his mother had two strokes within ten days. After the second stroke, it was apparent that she would need twenty-four-hour care. For various reasons, none of her children could have her live with them. Everyone was working, there was a lack of space in the apartments, and there was no elevator in the building in which her son was living. More than a year before his mother experienced the strokes, her son had applied for a Section VIII subsidy in order to move to another apartment, but he had not yet received approval.

Another resident who had a stroke experienced memory loss and also needed skilled nursing care after breaking her hip and her knee and experiencing another stroke during a convalescent stay at another nursing home.

Her daughter explained that she was placed in the nursing home because of her need for long-term skilled nursing care and also because she had a very large apartment that required a great deal of work.

Likewise, a Jewish resident was described by her sister as having many care needs following her stroke. She needed to use a wheelchair, had special dietary needs, needed twenty-four-hour care and physical therapy, and it was decided that she needed to be in the nursing home in order to receive more extensive physical therapy and other services. An alternative that was considered was a move to her niece's home, but her care needs were so extensive that this plan was not feasible. Additionally, her niece did not have adequate space for her, she would have been more isolated, and there would not have been much for her to do compared to the social and recreational opportunities available in a good nursing home.

Another Jewish resident was described as very debilitated and in need of physical therapy and other care after being hospitalized following a stroke, becoming ill with pneumonia, and experiencing relapses. His wife said she wanted to take him home after his rehabilitation in the nursing home, but he had "needed help with everything" when he was discharged from the hospital. Later it still would not have been possible for her to take him home because of his need for extensive care, especially because he could not walk well, and because of her own medical problems.

Likewise, the daughter of an African American resident who had experienced three strokes within a few weeks was told by her mother's doctor and the hospital social worker that her mother needed so much care that it would be too damaging for the daughter to bring her home and provide her care. Care would have been especially difficult because as a result of her paralysis, she needed to be lifted by two people.

For many of the African American residents, other medical problems resulted in admission. One resident needed a place to convalesce after a colostomy. Originally the placement was planned as temporary with the expectation that she would return home after the colostomy was reversed. After the reversal, she returned to the nursing home for rehabilitation but was very weak. She and her family decided that her general need for skilled nursing care was great and that the nursing home would be the best place for her to continue to receive the care she needed.

A woman with high blood pressure, circulatory problems, cardiac problems, and arthritis had been able to remain outside of a nursing home until she had a stroke. Her daughter thought she might have been able to remain at home with home care services except that two people were needed to lift her. A woman with diabetes and an ulcer had a stroke that affected her speech and another stroke a few months later that "knocked her out," according to her daughter, leaving her paralyzed. She needed twenty-four-hour care and could receive only four hours daily that was paid for by Medicaid. A woman described by her daughter as "so confused" had a stroke while in the hospital and was also diagnosed with Alzheimer's disease. She had been receiving assistance from a home attendant twelve hours daily for about three years, but her doctor and the hospital social worker thought that she needed more help after the stroke. She had been living with her daughter, who had many responsibilities because she was separated from her husband, rearing two young children, and working full-time, but she still did not want her mother to go into a nursing home.

Residents who entered the nursing home because of a physical problem other than a stroke often had experienced preexisting problems, but a specific incident generally occurred that resulted in the placement decision. Falls had precipitated placement for several of the residents, since after a fall the family had to confront potential dangers to the safety of the older relative in the home. A man who had arthritis and cardiac problems and who was experiencing weakness in his knees fell and was unable to open the door for his home attendant who came to help for five hours daily. He had stopped eating unless he was fed, did not have space for a home attendant to stay overnight to assist him, and was unable to receive twenty-four-hour home care on a daily basis. When he fell, his daughter decided that he should be admitted to a nursing home.

In another family, one day the wife of the resident had helped her husband into bed and then he got up for a cigarette and fell. He could not get up after his fall, and she was unable to get him up by herself, so she had to call the police to help. Her husband had paralysis on one side, and he had fallen many times. The family lived in a building without an elevator. A home attendant came to help six days a week, but he refused to let her provide any assistance.

People from each of the groups participating in the study shared many other experiences as well. An African American, a Jewish, and a Latino resident each fell at home and broke a hip. The African American resident's social worker had been unable to obtain adequate home care for him by the time he had been in the hospital for two months. He went into the nursing home after his application for twenty-four-hour home care was rejected by Medicaid. A Jewish resident became more disoriented after she was admitted to the hospital because of a broken hip. Her son did not believe that there were any workable alternatives to nursing home placement, since she was disoriented and needed rehabilitation for her broken hip. A Latina resident had been receiving twenty-four-hour home attendant services daily, but she fell and broke her hip while her home attendant was out. It had been difficult for her home attendant to take care of her because she had become forgetful and sometimes behaved very aggressively toward her. Another resident had a hip operation and then went into the nursing home for rehabilitation. The family considered the alternative of twenty-four-hour home care, but there was not enough space for a home attendant to stay in their home.

One Jewish and two African American residents entered the nursing home after being hospitalized for conditions related to amputations. Another Jewish resident arrived after being admitted to a hospital for an infection related to diabetes. He had already lost both of his legs as a result of the disease and had difficulty functioning in his apartment because it was hard to maneuver his wheelchair through the doorways.

Some African American residents who had had amputations developed various complications. A woman who had part of her leg and her foot amputated developed gangrene in her other leg. She was also hospitalized for triple bypass surgery. Another resident who was diabetic and had a leg amputated decided to go into the nursing home because she needed a great deal of assistance and lacked the requisite space for a twenty-four-hour home attendant. A resident whose foot had been amputated developed circulation problems in her other leg and had fallen several times at night.

Some of the Jewish residents experienced other problems. Before entering the nursing home, a resident stopped walking and needed twenty-four-hour care, but it was not feasible to continue to pay a great deal of money for home care. Another resident had a cardiac condition and had difficulty breathing. He could not take care of his needs and repeatedly called an ambulance to take him to the hospital. Because he did not want the home care that he was receiving, his doctor recommended that he go into a nursing home. A man with Parkinson's disease often called 911 when he felt weak, and he did not take his medications regularly. He was admitted to the nursing home after spending two weeks in the hospital, having been admitted because he felt weak. Though he had received home care, it had not met his needs adequately.

Several African American residents needed twenty-four-hour care and were unable to obtain this service. A woman had been taken to a hospital emergency room after she appeared to have a seizure. She developed paralysis and diabetes over the next month and needed round-the-clock care. Another resident needed a feeding tube and also needed extensive care twenty-four hours daily.

Difficulties in walking experienced by another resident became more severe when she developed a pinched nerve. She decided to go into the nursing home when she was in the hospital for treatment for high blood pressure. Another resident had several falls because she couldn't see, and her daughters decided that she should be admitted to the nursing home because she needed twenty-four-hour assistance. Her confusion may have also contributed to her falls.

RESIDENTS WITH PRIMARY DIAGNOSES
RELATED TO COGNITIVE FUNCTIONING

As indicated previously, twenty-two of the residents were admitted to the nursing home with a primary diagnosis related to cognitive loss. Cognitive losses had often developed over time; previous changes for these residents were described in chapter 4.

Several entered the nursing home from the hospital. The events that resulted in hospitalization for Latina/o residents included an attack on a resident by her home attendant; a resident falling twice in the same day; and a resident throwing herself from her bed to the floor. Among the Jewish residents, one woman had disappeared from her home. Another, whose deterioration in cognitive functioning had become apparent to her daughter six months before her hospitalization and admission to the nursing home, had gradually become more resistant to help. When neighbors reported that she was wandering outside naked she was taken to a hospital for evaluation and subsequently admitted to the nursing home. Among the African American residents, one was described as hallucinating before her admission to the nursing home. The wife of another decided that she could no longer provide adequate care at home after her husband went to bed fully clothed several times and would not let her help him undress.

Some of the residents who were diagnosed with cognitive losses moved directly into a nursing home from relatives' homes. A Latina who lived in her niece's home near the nursing home was wheeled in her wheelchair by her niece to the nursing home for her admission. Her niece had become concerned about her aunt's safety after she "threw herself from the bed and I knew she would get hurt." Medication had not calmed her adequately and, while some of the assistance from home attendants was good, one of her home attendants was unreliable. For one of the Jewish residents with cognitive loss who had twenty-four-hour care, the home care assistance was inconsistent, and the resident may also have been wandering late at night. A Latina who lived with her daughter needed care that included toileting and bathing, but she refused to use the toilet and she became very violent. Her daughter chose nursing home placement rather than applying for home care because she did not want her mother to experience the stress of the psychiatric evaluation that her mother's outpatient hospital social worker said would be required for home care. A Latina with Alzheimer's disease disappeared repeatedly from her daughter's home; her last disappearance lasted for three weeks. An African American resident also diagnosed with Alzheimer's disease lived with her daughter and had begun falling, was uncooperative at times, was up at night, and had become incontinent of bowels and urine. Her daughter said that her mother might have been able to remain at home if she had not become totally incontinent and if the family had the financial resources to provide twenty-four-hour home care assistance.

While some of the residents with dementia had exhibited irrational behavior contributing to the need for nursing home placement, other residents had psychological problems unrelated to dementia that precipitated their admission. A Latina became depressed, stopped eating and became dehydrated, and needed tube feeding four times each day. No relatives were available to help her with the tube feeding because they had to go to work, and therefore she went into the nursing home. She could not continue to live with her son because he was dying, and her daughter did not want her to witness his dying process. Her other relatives had small apartments, and so she could not move in with any of them. An African American woman was exhibiting paranoia and also had physical problems, including vision loss and other problems related to diabetes. She was also hostile to her home attendants, sending them away and refusing to eat. After a particularly hostile incident, she was taken to a hospital for psychiatric care and then admitted to the nursing home. Besides the difficulties involved in maintaining home care, many of her relatives were moving away from the community. Another African American resident had experienced psychological problems for many years but was able to function in the community with the help of her husband. After he died, however, she stopped taking her medications, was hospitalized, and entered the nursing home. Her sister could not take her into her home because of her own physical problems and the small size of her apartment.

PARTICIPATION IN THE DECISION-MAKING PROCESS

*I felt bad. I never knew how the nursing home worked. I thought no one would take
care of him.*   —A resident's wife, ten years after her husband's admission

The individuals involved in the decision-making process included the resident, relatives, friends, social workers, physicians, and others, but typically no more than three people made the final decision about each resident's
placement. By that time the individuals who were responsible were usually
in agreement about proceeding with the placement process. Sometimes
people who were not the actual decision makers, including the resident,
relatives, the resident's friends, or a social worker, disagreed. Usually the
person who became the primary family caregiver after the resident's admission was involved in making the placement decision.

For fourteen of the residents, the caregivers considered social workers to
have been participants in the decision-making process. Among the involved
social workers were the residents' hospital social workers, other hospital
social workers whom the residents' children knew, a social worker in the
housing development where a resident lived, a social worker affiliated with
a doctor's office, and a social worker at a community health center where a
resident's family received medical care.

One of the daughters said that her mother's hospital social worker was
not very helpful but that the social worker's supervisor helped. In another
family, when the resident needed to be discharged from the hospital, the social worker scheduled her for discharge to a nursing home that was not her
daughter's first choice without notifying her daughter prior to placement,
angering her daughter. Other relatives had failed to follow up, and the hospital wanted her to leave. One social worker's participation was described
as being limited to giving a relative a list of addresses and telephone numbers of nursing homes. In another family, relatives disagreed with a social
worker who wanted their father to go home with home attendant services
because they believed that he needed to go into a nursing home. They refused to take him home. For others, social workers were very helpful.

In one family, an attorney was involved in the decision-making process;
a conservator legally appointed to make decisions on her behalf was the sole
person involved in making the placement decision for another resident; and
an accountant who was a friend of the resident's daughter was involved in
decision making for another resident.

Only five of the seventy-five residents were identified as participating in the decision-making process. None of the Latina/o residents actually participated, but sixteen were told that they would be going to a nursing home. The relatives of three of these residents believed that they did not understand what they were told. Five residents were not given any information about where they were going, and relatives of two of those explained that they were not told because the relatives believed that they would not understand. Four were told directly that they were going to some other place, such as another hospital, not to a nursing home.

Among the African American and Afro-Caribbean residents, thirteen either were told that they were going to a nursing home or, in the case of three, were participants in the decision. One of the residents was told that she would be able to go home when the doctor said she could. One was told but did not understand, and another who was told understood "in a confused way." After arriving at the nursing home, a resident who had been told where she was going appeared to think that she was at home and that the nursing assistant was the home attendant who had assisted her before admission. Two of the residents were not told where they were going because it was believed that they would not understand because they had Alzheimer's disease.

Twelve Jewish residents knew that they were going to be living in a nursing home, and two of these individuals participated in making that decision. Five other Jewish residents were given the information, but they appeared either not to understand or not to remember. Five were told that they were going to a place where they would stay temporarily while receiving treatment or rehabilitation, and two were told that they were going to another hospital temporarily. One resident with Alzheimer's disease was not given any information about where she was going.

COMPARISON OF FINDINGS FROM THIS STUDY WITH OTHER RESEARCH FINDINGS ABOUT DECISION MAKING

Very few studies have addressed the process of decision making in nursing home placement, but the analyses by Bell (1996) and McAuley and Travis (1997) have generated findings similar to those in the Acacia study. Cicirelli's (1992) research exploring autonomy and paternalism in family decision making addressed issues that are different but related to areas explored in this study.

In her ethnographic study of the decision-making process of sixteen rural families with a relative who was admitted to a nursing home, Bell found
that variables influencing the decision-making process included whether the
placement was permanent or temporary, whether placement took place
from the resident's home or the hospital, and whether the older person was
involved in the decision. All of the elder and family participants in Bell's
study were rural Nebraska residents who were Caucasian, primarily of Ger-
man ancestry, and she believes that their ethnic background influenced their
attitudes about the placement process (Bell 2001).

Like the families described throughout this book, the families in Bell's
study experienced the decision for permanent placement as a crisis; nursing
home admission took place when family members believed that they could no
longer provide safe care or could not manage the required technical or physical labor of care. The findings also were similar in that caregivers had made
many interventions before placement. In Bell's study, placements expected
to be short term were not as traumatic, and several residents in Bell's study,
like some described in the Acacia study, believed that their stay was temporary although their relatives considered the placement to be permanent.

Also like most of the Acacia families, the primary family caregivers interviewed by Bell believed that involved family members had input into the
decision and that the family supported the decision. In Bell's study, the
caregivers believed that although they were the individuals who oversaw
implementation of the decision, the family had made the decision. In the
Acacia study, however, the primary caregiver usually indicated that only
one or two other people were the actual decision makers.

The family members in Bell's study who implemented the decision were
described as expressing "stress, guilt, and a sense of inadequate knowledge
and experience." Some participants in the Acacia study expressed similar
feelings. Bell also described residents who were able to participate actively
in locating the nursing home as being involved in the problem-solving
process, expressing their preferences, opinions, and wishes, and the Acacia
study included a few residents who had been similarly involved in their
own placement.

Regarding the role of health professionals in the decision, Bell described
some family members as satisfied with their participation. However, others
would have liked for physicians and other health care providers to be involved earlier by "identifying the need to place, helping them plan, providing anticipatory care, and supporting their decision" (Bell 1996:55). Some
relatives would have liked the doctor to discuss the need for placement with

the older adult who relatives thought needed to be admitted to a nursing home. Most of the families believed that the family was responsible for the decision and that they had the support of the doctor. When the resident was transferred from an acute care hospital to the nursing home, the doctor was considered a participant in the decision-making process because the doctor identified that as the right time and provided support. Some participants in the Acacia study described physicians as involved, but they generally did not speak of a doctor as one of the decision makers.

In Bell's study, as in the Acacia study, when the family members were asked about the role of other professionals in the decision for placement, social workers were the professionals most often mentioned as instrumental. Social workers provided assistance when residents were admitted to a nursing home directly from a hospital, at times answering questions and helping with paperwork, and they continued to be in contact after the move. In the Acacia study, no caregivers described further contact with a hospital social worker after placement occurred. The social workers in Bell's study told the relatives and future residents about the nursing home environment before placement and made arrangements for tours of the nursing homes. In the Acacia study, the relatives often contacted the nursing homes themselves to arrange for tours.

In Bell's study, the main priorities for the families in their selection of nursing homes were the care that would be provided and the cooperation and agreement of the resident with the decision. Cleanliness (absence of odors) was considered very important, and a close geographic location was also a priority. The ability to appreciate the resident as an individual and the provision of individualized care were considered very important by families. In the Acacia study, location was stated most frequently as the reason for choosing this nursing home, and recommendations, services, cleanliness, previous contact with the nursing home, and friendliness of staff were also important.

In another study, McAuley and Travis (1997) examined data from telephone interviews with 145 primary contact people (sponsors) who were most responsible for the decision-making process resulting in admission of a relative to a nursing home in Virginia. In their study, 17 percent of the sponsors were nonwhite, and all but one of the nonwhite sponsors were African American. The majority of the sponsors, 68 percent, were female; 66 percent were adult children or sons-in-law or daughters-in-law of the residents, 16 percent were spouses, 16 percent were other relatives, and 2 percent were friends. Fifty-three percent were employed, with 41 percent employed full-time and 12 percent part-time.

Besides the sponsors themselves, other people they considered to be very influential in the nursing home decision included physician (53 percent), social worker (39 percent), adult children of the resident (32 percent), family members besides spouse or adult children (32 percent), nurse (17 percent), and the resident (11 percent). According to the sponsors, spouses were the chief decision makers in 16 percent of the families but were not likely to be identified by other persons who were sponsors as influential. Lack of influence by a spouse might have occurred because there was no spouse or because the spouse was unable to participate. Adult children were more likely to be identified as very influential by adult child sponsors and sponsors who were spouses. A significant association was found between greater influence of a counselor or therapist and an adult child being more influential. Analysis of the relationship between resident characteristics and contextual factors and the residents' level of influence suggested that when residents were viewed by sponsors as more oriented at the time of the decision they were more influential in the decision. They were also considered more influential when they had recently been hospitalized or when sponsors experienced higher levels of competing demands at the time when the decision was being made.

Social workers and nurses were more influential in the decision-making process when the sponsor was a person of color and when a physician was more involved. Social workers and physicians were more influential when hospitalization was a factor in the decision. A nurse was more influential when the resident was disoriented or confused at the time the decision was being made. In the Acacia study, none of the caregivers identified a nurse as having an influential role in the decision-making process.

Another perspective has been offered by Victor Cicirelli (1992) on the basis of his research on mother-daughter dyads. Autonomy and paternalism in decision making were not direct focuses of the Acacia research, but comparisons to some of the findings of Cicirelli's study can be made. According to Cicirelli, although autonomy is an important value in family caregiving, at times autonomy is appropriate and at other times it is not. Cicirelli also noted that the autonomy of other adults may be either enhanced or diminished by the actions of family members and professional caregivers. Cicirelli's goals were to predict who would be the decision maker and whether the outcome would be a paternalistic decision or a decision that respected the autonomy of the older adult. Both of these variables would influence effective decision making pertaining to caregiving tasks and provide feedback about the relationship, according to Cicirelli.

In his theory of dyadic family caregiving decision making, Cicirelli (1992:58) developed a structural theory, concerned with an aspect of the relationship between the members of the dyad themselves, in which "outcomes related only to contextual and personal-social variables." The relationship exhibits unique characteristics in that it usually involves care of an aging family member with varying degrees of dependency and a long history that may include extensive caregiving and care receiving within dyads. It is important to "understand the antecedents that determine the agent of decision making and the consequences for effective decision making, as well as any ethical concerns with what 'ought to be'" (Cicirelli 1992:52).

Cicirelli suggested that a family caregiving decision-making system is hierarchical and semiautonomous. The interacting component parts do not have the same impact on each other, and sometimes they "may have little or no effect upon the total system." According to Cicirelli, the adult daughter–elderly mother relationship is a basic dyadic unit in the total family caregiving decision-making system, but other family members may also have a secondary impact on caregiving and decision making. At times, however, other family members may have no impact because they have little or no interaction with a semiautonomous dyad. Cicirelli suggests that the existence of semiautonomous portions of the family system supports his decision to select the mother-daughter dyad as the basic caregiving decision-making unit and to search for antecedent factors influencing autonomous and paternalistic decision making within the mother-daughter dyad. He also believes that semiautonomous functioning of dyads can justify studying the dyad as relatively independent from both the family system and the larger systems that are external to the family. This approach limits the factors that are studied to characteristics of the daughter and mother themselves in order to determine whether these characteristics are antecedents of autonomous and paternalistic decision making.

In the Acacia study, however, many other relatives, in addition to the daughters caring for their mothers, had a primary role in decision making regarding their relative's admission to the nursing home. These others included sons, husbands, wives, sisters-in-law, daughters-in-law, nephews, nieces, cousins, grandsons, and granddaughters. Discussion among family members usually took place, but the final decision was made by individuals who included the primary caregivers, seemingly based on the belief that the caregiver should have a major role in the decision-making process because he or she was most affected by the problems that led to consideration of nursing home admission.

In the Acacia study, the primary caregiver and the person receiving care could not always be considered a semiautonomous dyad. In some families, they clearly could not; in others, the semiautonomous dyad did exist, but it was not always composed of a mother and a daughter. Findings in the Acacia study suggest that mothers and daughters cannot be assumed to always constitute semiautonomous dyads in terms of decision making or other tasks and that other dyads cannot be assumed to not be semiautonomous.

Cicirelli identified key variables that were common predictors in the relationships between mothers and daughters in his study. He determined that the mother was more likely to make autonomous decisions if the attitude of the daughter was less negative toward elderly people in general, if the daughter had weaker attachment to her mother, if the daughter had a higher level of education, and if the mother was younger. Conversely, daughters were more likely to make paternalistic decisions if they had a more negative attitude toward elderly people in general, a greater attachment to their mothers, less education, and older mothers. Cicirelli suggests that his findings indicate that culture and socialization contributing to attitudes about older adults may influence beliefs about autonomy and paternalism held by adult children and elderly parents, and he recommends educating caregiving daughters on general topics and on the abilities and strengths of older adults. It is also true, however, that research focusing upon informal caregiving by other persons suggests that education in these areas is important for other caregivers as well as for daughters.

The Acacia study suggests that cultural expectations are likely to play an important role in autonomous and paternalistic decision making within families regarding nursing home placement. Cultural values may preclude older adults with more traditional values choosing nursing home placement, whereas younger relatives experiencing demands may choose nursing home placement (Kolb 1999; Kolb 2000).

Cicirelli (1992) found that congruence between family members on topics related to decision making was moderate at best. Even when family members know, or think they know, the older relative's wishes, their decision may be paternalistic, made according to what they think is best for their relative rather than that person's desires. Therefore, Cicirelli recommends better communication between parents and their adult children so that the children will clearly understand their parent's wishes well in advance. Nevertheless, as Cicirelli has suggested, autonomous decision making is not always best. Findings in the Acacia study support the idea that even when the older person's preference to stay out of a nursing home has clearly been stated throughout his or her lifetime, autonomous decision making may not be allowed if there are compelling health reasons for placement and the older person's attitude does not change.

Cicirelli suggested that parents choose adult children as surrogates on the basis of trust and confidence that they share the same beliefs and values. The quality of the relationship appears to take precedence over whether the decision is made according to a parent's wishes or according to what the children think is best. Cicirelli reaches the interesting conclusion that the older generation believed more strongly in paternalism, although the generations shared similar beliefs about independent and shared autonomy. A preference for paternalism appeared to operate if it would ensure the welfare, health, and safety of the older relative.

According to Cicirelli, it is important to facilitate intergenerational congruence in a caregiving situation so that those involved will be more willing to work together and thereby avoid conflict. He suggests that the lack of congruence may be related to discontinuity in socialization between generations in contemporary times. As indicated previously, and as findings in the Acacia study illustrate, the attitudes of different cohorts may develop under very different social circumstances.

EMOTIONAL REACTIONS TO THE PLACEMENT DECISION

I was sad; if she had the choice she wouldn't want to come to the nursing home. At home, she was independent.

—A resident's daughter, six months after her mother's admission

Emotional reactions of the future Acacia Nursing Home residents and their relatives varied greatly within each group. Among the African American residents who were told that they were going to a nursing home and understood what that meant, one daughter said that the decision made her feel sad and described her mother, the resident, as resigned, as were other family members. In another family, a man who entered the nursing home felt bad about it, but his wife felt good because her husband would receive the care that he needed. Likewise, the niece of a resident felt good about the decision, and her aunt, who was involved in making the decision, also felt good about it because it would mean that she would be able to receive care that she needed. In another family, a resident's cousin felt bad about the decision but did not believe that there was any other choice, and the resident, who was very independent and had wanted to go into a nursing home when he could no longer take care of his needs himself, felt good about it. The son of a Jewish resident described the experience as "a sad time in her and my life" but realized that his mother was quite relieved. Likewise, the niece of a Puerto Rican resident felt bad about it, but both she and her aunt were comfortable with the decision. The brother of another Puerto Rican resident said that he was glad about the decision, and his sister was agreeable to nursing home placement because she understood that she needed care and believed that it was not a good idea to rely on neighbors any longer.

Emotional responses in families in which residents were told that they were going to a place other than a nursing home varied. An African American daughter who told her mother that she was going to a hospital felt bad about the decision to place her mother in the nursing home. Her mother became very agitated when she was taken to the home and was concerned about where she was. A daughter who told her mother that she was going to a hospital described the decision as unpleasant, and her mother never told her how she felt about it. The third African American daughter who told her mother that she was going to a hospital said that her mother was not completely aware of what was happening and insisted for the first several months that she was going home. Her daughter and other relatives had expected that her mother would return home, and the daughter had felt happy about the decision that her mother would go to the nursing home. A Jewish resident who thought she was going to another hospital for a temporary stay was happy because she was leaving the hospital, where she had been unhappy, but her son felt guilty. Another Jewish resident had been told that he was going to a rehabilitation center, and he was feeling depressed and generally negative about everything. His wife felt bad about the decision and hoped that his functioning would improve enough for him to return home.

The responses were also quite varied among several Latina residents who were told that they were going to a "place." A daughter told her mother that she was going to a place and that after she went to work she would come back for her, and her mother appeared to accept that explanation. Another resident was told by her son that she needed to go to a "special place" that was not the same as a nursing home. She was unhappy with this idea and wanted to remain at home but realized that she could not do so. Many Latina/o residents and their relatives experienced very strong emotional reactions to the placement decision (Kolb 1999). A daughter felt that she was abandoning her father; he was very angry and said, "Well, if you want to get me out of the house." Another daughter said that she felt guilty because she had never thought that she would place her mother in a nursing home, but she also felt relieved because she would know where her mother was when she was working. However, her mother was angry about it and cursed at her. Another woman said that when she told her husband that he would need to go to a nursing home he did not believe it at first. When he realized that this was going to happen, he was very angry, and his wife felt very bad.

TRANSITIONAL NURSING HOME PLACEMENTS

One difficulty in the placement process for some of the residents and their families was that the resident was admitted to another nursing home before transfer to the permanent nursing home. Most of the interim placements were for less than three months. Interim placements occurred most frequently for Latina/o residents, affecting ten of them despite the fact that many of the Latina/o families strongly preferred placement at Acacia Nursing Home. In contrast, only one of the African American residents had experienced a transitional placement, and two Jewish residents had experienced earlier placements, but these were long-term placements outside of this area. In all of the groups, there were family members who felt pressured by hospital staff to place their relative in a nursing home rapidly, but in the African American, Afro-Caribbean, and Jewish families their relative was more often transferred directly to Acacia.

The reasons for the greater number of Latina/o residents with transitional placements are not entirely clear. Several factors may be relevant. A greater number of Latino families preferred that admission be to this specific nursing home because relatives lived nearby. In contrast, more families in the other groups may have found placement in other homes satisfactory because location within a larger geographic area was considered acceptable. Therefore, African American, Afro-Caribbean, and Jewish families whose relative was admitted to another nursing home may have been less likely to request transfer to this nursing home. Second, fewer Latino families had any previous experience with a relative's nursing home admission, and their lack of experience may have made it more difficult to exercise control in relation to the systems that were involved. Third, Acacia requires that all of the necessary paperwork be completed before admission, whereas some nursing homes in this city do not operate with that requirement. Therefore, even if a bed is available in both nursing homes, an applicant may need to go to a home that is not the first choice because that home will accept the person without completion of paperwork. If the applicant and family continue to want placement in that home after admission elsewhere, a transfer may take place after all paperwork is completed and a bed is available. Fourth, Latino families may have had different experiences because of differences in discharge policies among hospitals. Finally, Latino families may have been treated differently because of subjective reactions, for unknown reasons, on the part of hospital staff. The high proportion of transitional placements among the Latina/o residents may have been the result of any of these factors, some combination of them, or other factors not yet identified.

REASONS FOR CHOOSING ACACIA NURSING HOME

While African American, Jewish, and Latino families shared many of the same reasons for their choice, in some cases important differences existed in the number of families in each group indicating a specific reason. Although location was stated most frequently by members of each group as a reason, Latina/o relatives were most likely to indicate that they preferred Acacia because relatives or the resident lived in the neighborhood. Fifteen of the Latina/o participants gave this reason, while nine of the Jewish and five of the African American participants also did so. One of the Latina/o participants said that Acacia was chosen because it was in this part of the city, and another said that it was chosen because it was difficult to find a nursing home in Puerto Rico. A Jewish participant gave the reason that it was in this particular city. Three African American daughters chose it because it was near their place of employment. Four African American relatives or friends responded that it was in a good location, and one of them described it as being in a central location. Four Jewish relatives identified the home as being in a good location, as did one Latina.

Although location was the most frequently stated reason, many others were also mentioned. Recommendations by a broad variety of people were important to the decision-making process in several families. Latina/o caregivers indicated most frequently that they had heard people talking about it or that people had recommended it. Seven Latina/o relatives said this, as well as four Jewish and two African American participants. African American families were most likely to indicate that recommendation of this nursing home by hospital social workers was important in the decision, and three African American relatives said that a recommendation by a physician was important. Relatives of three Latinas considered recommendation by a hospital social worker to be important in the decision, as did one Jewish relative. Two Latinas and one other Jewish relative considered recommendation of the home by a physician to be important. Others who recommended the home included a member of the home's board of directors, an attorney, a relative or friend working at the home, a community social worker who was a former employee, a relative or friend who was a resident, a friend whose mother was a resident, and the organization Friends and Relatives of the Institutionalized Aged (FRIA). Another family decided to consider the home after hearing about it on a radio program.

A small number of people in each group indicated that the services provided by the home were a reason for choosing Acacia over others. Physical therapy, the general quality of care, and cleanliness were mentioned in services-related responses. The friendliness of the staff working in the nursing home was important in the decision of two caregivers, as were positive feelings about the admissions social worker for two other people. One caregiver also considered contact with the admissions social worker to be important in the decision, and a follow-up call from an admissions social worker was important in the decision of another person.

Two relatives attributed their decision to the good reputation of the home, and another considered the home's affiliation with a major teaching hospital to be an important factor. A Latina daughter preferred the home because of her admiration for Jewish people and their care of their families. Four relatives simply said that it felt right, was "the least of all evils," or they liked it.

Ten families had had previous contact with this nursing home that influenced their decision. This contact included participation by four residents in the adult day program operated by the nursing home, a resident's history of employment at Acacia, and previous residence by relatives of three of the Latina/o residents and two Jewish residents.

Finally, it is important that, at a time when hospital staff feel pressured to discharge patients rapidly, very few caregivers said that the family decided that the resident would go to this nursing home because it had the first bed available and so admission could take place right away. Only one Latino, two African American, and two Jewish families gave bed availability as a reason for choosing Acacia. Bed availability may, however, be an explanation for transitional placements of several Latina residents, in which they went to another nursing home upon discharge from a hospital and later transferred to Acacia.

Besides being asked why the residents came to this specific nursing home, the relatives and friends were asked how they felt about the home during the application process and whether there was anything that they especially liked or disliked at the time. The application process usually included a tour of the nursing home conducted by a staff member in the Social Work Department, a meeting with a social worker, and completion of required paperwork.

The characteristics that participants from each group said they especially liked during the application process were cleanliness of the facilities and friendliness of staff. Six African American, nine Jewish, and seven Latino relatives mentioned cleanliness, while twelve African American, four Jewish, and four Latino relatives and friends listed friendliness. In addition to saying that they especially liked the friendliness of staff, African American relatives and friends also said that it was important that staff members were caring and reassuring and took time with them. Four Jewish and two African American relatives said that they especially liked the social or therapeutic activities or services. Other relatives liked musical activities, medical services, and the coffee shop; proximity to hospitals; the resident's roommate; attractiveness of rooms and spaciousness of the nursing home; lack of restraints; the library and the arts and crafts program; the large number of volunteers; quality of care; security; and affiliation with the Jewish agencies federation.

Except for one relative who indicated that she disliked the general situation, African American relatives and friends did not indicate anything that they disliked during the application process. A Latina said that she felt depressed, and two other Latinas said that it bothered them to see the sick residents. Similarly, three of the Jewish relatives disliked the fact that the nursing home is an institution and said that they disliked seeing sick people; two relatives were concerned about security, another relative believed that there was a lack of stimulation, and another thought that the amount of time allocated to the discussion and tour was too short.

SOCIAL CHANGE AND DECISION MAKING ABOUT CARE NEEDS OF OLDER ADULTS AND THEIR FAMILIES

The aging and society paradigm described in chapter 1 proposes that changes in individuals' lives influence and are influenced by changes in social structures and institutions (Riley, Foner, and Riley 1999). The paradigm addresses aging as a lifelong biopsychosocial process that is closely related to social structures. Experiences earlier in life that are related to the biopsychosocial makeup of individuals can have long-term consequences over the course of a lifetime. Age operates within social structures as "a criterion, or set of expectations or norms . . . for entering and leaving particular structures, for performing roles in these structures, and for access to the associated resources (such as money, prestige, or power)" (Riley, Foner, and Riley 1999:332).

An important concept from the paradigm that is relevant to the information presented in this chapter is the dynamic nature of aging. The concept of cohort differences addresses this concept—the idea that members of different cohorts age in different ways because of changes that occur in societies. For many of the families in this study, the resident was the first family member to live in a nursing home, and only a few residents had any relatives who had previously lived in a nursing home.

When the relationship between social change and changes in patterns of people's lives is considered, the paradigm proposes interdependence and asynchrony between these dynamisms. Information from participants in this study about the reasons for their decision to seek nursing home placement reveals societal changes that have influenced changes in patterns of the lives of older adults and their families. Physical and cognitive illnesses that resulted in the need for greater care than the family could provide reflected the trend toward increased life expectancy in the United States and the increasing prevalence of debilitating illnesses as people reach old age, an experience more likely to occur among older adults in this cohort than among those of previous cohorts. In addition, cohort changes were reflected in the lack of availability of informal caregivers, female and male, because they were employed and could not terminate their employment. In many families, formal services that were needed to supplement the care that relatives and friends could provide were unavailable, unaffordable, or inadequate, reflecting asynchrony and resulting in imbalances between what the families and residents needed and expected and what was offered by social structures.

One of the important considerations is that nursing homes have continued to develop and expand to meet care needs, but a nursing home is not always the option preferred by older adults in need of care or by their relatives and friends. As indicated in the earlier discussion of structural lag, although lives have been changing in the United States, compensatory structural changes have lagged far behind, resulting in strains on individuals and on society in general (Riley and Riley 1986). Many of the participants preferred that care be provided at home. If affordable home care, therapeutic services, and accessible, affordable housing had been available, some of the residents might have been able to remain at home longer. Nursing homes need to be available for older adults who are unable to remain at home even when comprehensive services are available, but some of the residents and families in this study would have chosen to continue care at home if the formal service system had been able to help them meet their needs. While Riley and her colleagues have emphasized the failure of the United States to provide adequate opportunities in education, family, and work for growing numbers of healthy older persons, the experiences of families in this study support the view that society has also failed to provide adequate resources for care and support for older adults and their families when they experience difficulties and need assistance.

Findings from this study indicate that residents and their families across all groups shared many experiences related to decision making and placement, and some of these experiences are also reflected in findings of other research studies. Family members made very difficult decisions based upon their assessments of the resident's and the caregivers' needs and the options that they perceived to be available. The placement decision involved consideration of changes in the physical, cognitive, and/or psychological functioning of the older adult and situational factors such as inadequate options for care at home and lack of housing appropriate for the resident's needs. Many of the families' experiences demonstrate that structural lag exists in the failure to develop an adequate array of options to maintain older adults at home when this is preferred by families and is feasible in terms of care needs. Among the problematic issues in the areas of home care and housing were the high cost of living in this city and difficulties that families experience at times in securing adequate home care services, even if they are eligible for Medicaid. In contrast to the difficulties experienced in obtaining adequate home care, the services needed by nursing home residents were reimbursed when residents became eligible for Medicaid.

Residents frequently did not participate in the decision-making process, but relatives and professionals were often involved. Some of the residents were unable to understand the need for placement, but their general lack of participation suggests a need for professional intervention to assist relatives and friends in exploring and addressing concerns regarding participation of residents in the process and in facilitating that participation.

Service providers, residents, and families also need to address the circumstances that lead to transitional placements for residents and identify any contributing factors. Residents and their informal caregivers need assistance in becoming empowered in placement planning in order to make optimum arrangements.

Information from this study shows that professionals in hospitals, the community, agencies, and nursing homes assume important roles as providers of information and support to older adults and their relatives and friends in the decision-making and application process. This assistance is needed and valued during a time that is often experienced as a crisis. Some relatives regarded their positive contact with social workers and other nursing home staff as influential in the decision to place the resident in Acacia Nursing Home.

6

SETTLING IN:
ADJUSTING TO THE CHANGES

I felt terrible because he didn't want to stay.
> —A resident's wife, ten years after her husband's admission

They greeted us with open arms, and they still do.
> —A resident's friend, one year after her friend's admission

I feel good. There wouldn't have been anybody to take care of him at home. It would have been worse. At the beginning, I felt really, really bad.
> —A resident's granddaughter, three years after her grandfather's admission

THE EXPERIENCES leading to admission had been difficult for residents and for their relatives and friends, but finally the day to move into the nursing home had arrived. This chapter addresses the final phase of the transit stage, admission day; the process of resettlement, or adjustment to life in the nursing home, including issues of ethnicity and provision of services; and reflections of relatives and friends about the placement decision and plans for the future.

Adapting Drachman and Ryan's stage-of-migration framework to the events taking place after admission, the discussion of the resettlement process for residents and their relatives and friends begins in this chapter and continues in chapters 7 and 8. Drachman and Ryan identify critical variables in the resettlement stage for immigrants migrating to another country, including cultural issues, reception from the host country, opportunity structure of the host country, discrepancy between expectations and reality, and the degree of cumulative stress experienced throughout the migration process. In applying the resettlement concept to adjustment to a nursing home, the salient variables become adjustment of residents and their relatives and friends to nursing home culture, services and other support provided by staff, social and recreational opportunities provided by the nursing home, discrepancies between the expectations of residents and their relatives and friends and the realities of nursing home life, and the degree of cumulative stress resulting from experiences before placement, the admissions process, and adjustment to life in the nursing home.

ADMISSION DAY

The Move Into the Nursing Home

They were doing a lot of things to her right away, and I was glad that they were doing what she needed.

—A resident's daughter, ten months after her mother's admission

Most of the seventy-five residents in this study were accompanied by the relative or friend who was interviewed or were met by that person when they arrived at the nursing home. Generally the contact of residents and their relatives and friends with staff on that day was positive and consistent with expectations of the responsibilities of staff on the day that residents are admitted. Social workers, nurses, doctors, nursing assistants, and orderlies met the residents and the family members and friends who were present. In general, the study participants viewed this initial contact as a satisfactory experience. They described staff as welcoming, friendly, very nice, good without an exception, ready, and practical.

The son of a Jewish resident said that the staff treated his mother and family members nicely; he felt that she was in a comfortable place and he was reassured when his mother was given a physical exam right away. She fell on the first day, and "they didn't go nuts." The nurse took care of her. The niece of an African American resident described a head nurse as wonderful, and it was important to her that the nurse said that she would take care of her aunt. Likewise, the wife of a Latino resident said that the nurse assured her that they would take care of her husband, asked what he liked to eat and do, and spoke to him directly. The daughter of a Latino resident said that the orderly introduced himself and was very friendly and that "it made me feel like he was in the right place."

Some relatives described negative experiences. For example, the daughter of a Jewish resident believed that emotional support for her mother was inadequate and also said that she had an argument with a nurse about her mother's medications. The daughter of an African American resident said that a few of the professionals could have been nicer, and the wife of a Jewish resident said that the staff was sort of indifferent. A Latina said that staff did not give enough respect to her mother, the resident's wife. A Latino son said that it bothered him that his mother's roommate was very ill and also that there were no people on her unit who spoke Spanish.

In their interviews, caregivers were asked if there was anything that would have helped them to feel more comfortable. Although fifty-four said they could not think of anything, others had specific recommendations. Some of the ideas pertained to circumstances that may be uncomfortable for some incoming residents and their relatives and friends but may generally be beyond the control of the nursing home staff. Some relatives would have liked for the resident to be in a room or on a floor with people who were healthier, but the reality was that often only one bed was available at any given time and no other option for a room existed. Residents were admitted to the floor where their needs could be most adequately met, so if they appeared likely to need long-term care it was unlikely that they would be placed on the short-term rehabilitation floor where there were people who were not as ill.

Other recommendations included receiving written information before admission about what to expect on the first day, emotional support and warmth, more attention, more formal welcoming by a receiving committee/staff, respect for residents and relatives, and the opportunity to talk with a social worker just as they had been able to talk in this research interview. Another recommendation was that the initial reception be conducted in a quiet place other than the room where the resident would be living.

Emotional Reactions

I can't believe what I was doing for her. It was so hard I went home and cried.
        —A resident's daughter, nine months after her mother's admission

Relatives and friends of the residents described their own reactions to admission in various ways, with Latina/o caregivers describing the most discomfort. A Latina whose grandfather was admitted said, "It was sad to leave him here; everything was sad." In describing her feelings about the experience, a wife said, "I felt terrible because he didn't want to stay." A daughter said, "When I had to depart from him that day, that wasn't no good. I felt like I was neglecting him." However, she knew that he would receive the care he needed. A granddaughter said that in her family relatives were "responsible for our own" and so "the transition was difficult." She felt like she was "giving her away to a stranger" and felt guilty because her grandmother had taken care of her relatives but now was being placed in a nursing home herself.

In contrast, some of the Latinas/os were less distressed. A son said that he felt good because he knew that his father would be in a clean environment and that the nurses and doctors would take care of him. The experience was also described as "normal" and as "all right." For some, the positive feelings at Acacia were related to negative experiences with a nursing home from which the relative had been transferred and the impression that this home was better. Caregivers of African American, Afro-Caribbean, and Jewish residents generally did not describe themselves as emotionally upset on admissions day.

Although many of the caregivers did not view themselves as distressed that day, when asked whether they or their relative had felt depressed about the nursing home placement and how the depression was experienced, many said that the resident and they themselves were depressed by the placement. Several Latina/o caregivers felt depressed at the time of the placement, though the feelings diminished after a while. A daughter said that she felt depressed "at the beginning, but now I feel I got no choice." Another daughter said that she felt depressed for about a week and then decided that she just had to accept it. Sometimes she felt depressed again if her mom had problems. A niece said that she felt depressed in the first weeks. The wife of a resident who had been in the home for ten years said that she had felt depressed, but not for a long time. She said, "Later I started understanding; I saw he was clean." A son and daughter felt depressed because they were worried since they had learned about problems in nursing homes from television. They felt better after they visited and saw that everything was fine. A granddaughter said that she felt depressed and still felt sad three years later. Another daughter said that she felt depressed and guilty. A daughter said that she felt depressed, that her mother was blaming her, but the situation had improved. A daughter said that her sisters and she had felt depressed, that it had been so difficult to give up their mother's apartment. A son said that he had felt a little bad, but not depressed. A daughter whose father had been at the nursing home for only two months said that sometimes she feels like crying. Some caregivers, however, described themselves as either sad or depressed after longer periods of time. A daughter said that she still feels depressed, especially after she visits her mother.

Jewish caregivers also experienced feelings of depression, sadness, and guilt. A resident's nieces felt guilty, one of them because she had promised her aunt that she would never be in a nursing home. In another family, the niece felt guilty about her uncle's placement. A resident's wife described herself as depressed because she felt guilty. A nephew described his aunt's relatives as a little sad, resigned. A resident's wife said that she felt depressed but had hoped her husband's stay in the nursing home would be temporary and that he would return home. As did some of the Latina/o relatives, some Jewish caregivers' depressed feelings experienced at the time of admission abated as time elapsed. A resident's sister said that family members were depressed about what had happened but began to feel better when they saw her well taken care of and involved in activities. A resident's brother felt depressed for a few weeks.

Some of the relatives of Jewish residents had not been depressed. A resident's sister-in-law said that she was not depressed, that she was accepting of the placement because her sister was ninety-two when she was admitted. The niece of a resident who was admitted after a stroke said that family members were not depressed. The relatives of a resident whose long-term depression lifted after her admission to the nursing home were not depressed, nor was the daughter of a resident who was relieved to see people and was not depressed herself. The sons of a resident who could spend time with his wife, who was also a resident, were not depressed.

Among the caregivers of African American and Afro-Caribbean residents, some experienced depression, sadness, and anxiety, though none said that they had felt guilty. A daughter who was very sad about her mother's need for placement explained, "All the things she [the mother] likes to do she can't do now." Another daughter was anxious about what the outcome of placement would be and was worried about what she would do if her mother was discharged. She originally thought that her mother's placement would be short term, but after two years she believed that her mother would be in the nursing home permanently. Likewise, a resident's niece had been concerned about how it would turn out. A niece said that the placement experience increased her depression because of the overwhelming newness of the situation. A resident's wife said, "I had to get used to it. Sometimes I'd wake up at two o'clock and think he was in the other bed."

Some caregivers of African American and Afro-Caribbean residents did not describe uncomfortable feelings regarding the placement. A resident's friend said that she did not feel depressed, since she believed that her friend would be taken care of around the clock. Likewise, a resident's sister said that she was not depressed, since she believed that her sister would receive the needed care. A resident's cousin said that she had put the pieces together and knew that "you can't question God. This is where you have to go with life." A daughter said that she had not been depressed because work did not allow it.

Although some caregivers believed that they did not know the emotional reactions of their relative or friend who was admitted, others were confident that they did. Some of the African American residents were described as depressed following admission. However, caregivers of some African American and Afro-Caribbean residents believed that their relatives' emotional reactions to admission were influenced by cognitive loss. For example, a daughter said that her mother was not depressed but that she was "at the stage of not knowing where she was" and was asking where she was. Although her daughter thought that this confusion occurred because of cognitive loss, it is also possible that her mother's confusion may have been exacerbated because she had been told that she was going to the hospital rather than to a nursing home. Some emotional reactions may also have been a result of expectations about life in the nursing home; a resident described by her friend as depressed had said before admission that "she didn't think she was going to like it." It was difficult to determine the emotional reactions of some of the residents because of their personality characteristics; for example, the daughter of one woman said that her mother was not the type to cry or complain. Some residents were depressed, but not about admission to the nursing home. A woman who had been "a bit independent" appeared to be depressed about the amputation of her foot rather than about the move to the nursing home.

Some African American and Afro-Caribbean residents felt better after admission. A resident who was "feeling down" while she was in the hospital felt better after her transfer to the nursing home. Another resident "just wanted to live" and was glad that she was getting better. A resident's wife said that her husband was not depressed, that there were many women in the nursing home and that he was "a female's man." The daughter of another resident believed that it was helpful that the family kept her mother occupied by their visits.

Some Jewish residents were also very depressed, but one was described as elated, particularly because she was glad to leave the hospital. One of the residents was relieved to be with people. Another was pleased that he would be able to see his wife regularly since she was already a resident of the nursing home. Still another was not depressed but just wanted to go home. The niece of one resident described her aunt as not having room to feel depressed about her placement because she was angry and upset about a lot of things. One resident was described as always having been depressed. Among the Jewish residents, as with the African American and Afro-Caribbean residents, cognitive impairment was also believed to affect the emotional responses to admission.

Emotional reactions of Latina/o residents also varied greatly. As in the African American and Afro-Caribbean and Jewish groups, the degree of cognitive impairment seemed to affect Latinas/os' reactions to admission. A resident's niece said that the reason her aunt was not depressed was because her cognitive loss reduced her understanding. In addition, impaired speech made it difficult to assess the emotional reactions of some residents, but nonverbal communication could provide clues. The daughter of an aphasic resident saw a tear come out of her mother's eye.

Residents' reactions to their admission included anger, depression, "feeling badly," acceptance, desire to return home, and lack of understanding that they were being admitted to a nursing home. A niece who had not been able to bring herself to tell her aunt that she was going to a nursing home told her that she was going to the hospital for an appointment, and when they arrived at the nursing home her aunt "started screaming and screaming." A daughter said that her mother was angry and "cried a lot and said take me home please" although her daughter believed that she did not understand that she was at a nursing home. Another daughter said that her father felt bad and started crying. Relatives described a husband, a father, and a mother as angry.

Relatives thought that the depression of some of the Latina/o residents was caused by something other than admission to the nursing home. One resident was depressed about her son's ill health. A daughter said that her mother was never a person to be "enclosed" and that she was depressed because she was "enclosed" in the nursing home. As with the caregivers, some residents were depressed only at the beginning of their stay. The wife of a resident said that after a year her husband stopped fighting her about being in the nursing home. A resident who was sad felt better at a later time. Some residents had been depressed at a previous nursing home but were no longer depressed after they transferred to this home. Likewise, two residents were described as depressed at home but as less depressed or not depressed at the nursing home.

RESETTLEMENT

Expectations and Realities

Now we know it's not how it looks on TV and how people think. It's better.
—A resident's granddaughter, three years after her grandfather's admission

Interviews with the relatives and friends of the residents took place between two months and ten years after the resident's admission to Acacia, and fifty-three of the residents participating in the study had lived in the nursing home for at least one year before the interview. Asked about whether the experience of having their relative in the nursing home had been different from their expectations, relatives of fifteen African American and Afro-Caribbean residents replied that the experience did not differ from their expectations, while five said that it was better than expected and four said that they had not known what to expect. One remarked that the home was much cleaner than many. Expectations had been shaped partially by negative reports in the media about nursing homes, but more positive expectations had resulted from relatives' employment in nursing homes, visiting the home before admission, and knowing people with relatives who were residents in this home.

Likewise, twelve of the Jewish relatives said that the experience was similar to their expectations, and seven said they had not known what to expect or were not certain what they had expected, while two indicated that it was better than expected. Other participants did not know how to respond or provided other information, noting either that the experience had been difficult but the staff was good or that it had been helpful not to have to bear the complete responsibility for providing care.

Among the Latina/o relatives, eleven found the nursing home to be as they expected, two either had not been sure what to expect or did not know what they had expected, and nine believed that the experience at the home was better than they had expected. For one daughter, the experience was not as good as she had expected, and a few participants did not indicate their expectations. This was the group most likely to report that the experience was better than expected, and participants responded that it was different from what they had heard on television, better than residents' previous nursing homes, and better than the nursing home in which one participant worked. The Latina/o residents were also less likely to have a relative who had previously been placed in a nursing home.

Ethnicity and Provision of Services

It would give her comfort if she could know it [the nursing home] was Jewish.
—A resident's nephew, four years after his aunt's admission

For some of the African American and Afro-Caribbean, Jewish, and Latina/o relatives and residents, there were significant experiences in the nursing home related to ethnicity and race. Some of these experiences were positive and others were negative, but most of the relatives and friends believed that the needs of the residents for whom they were caregivers were adequately met. Concerns about food, hair care, language, the need to show respect to older relatives, and religious services were identified. However, when asked whether the resident, family, and friends had been treated fairly, most of the relatives and friends stated that they themselves had been treated fairly, and most also believed that the residents had been treated fairly.

Issues pertaining to food were especially important for some of the African American, Jewish, and Latina/o residents and their families. The granddaughter of an African American resident noted, "You don't get the kind of food you used to get." Kosher-style or Jewish food was mentioned as being important to some of the Jewish residents, and food was mentioned by Latina/o caregivers as important to residents. Relatives pointed out that residents had been used to eating Spanish food their entire lives and liked that kind of food, and some relatives had considered it important to bring rice and beans or Spanish coffee to residents. As noted in chapter 2, Dobrof (1977) observed a cultural and ethnic pattern of families providing special foods to Jewish, Italian, British West Indian, Irish, and black residents in her study, and findings in the Acacia study regarding Latina/o family caregivers' provision of food are consistent with this pattern.

Other issues that were important to some of the African American residents and their relatives included the need for Protestant religious services weekly rather than every other week; as indicated previously, some of the

African American residents had been very active in their churches, even to the extent of being "the mother of her church." The other issue that was raised was the need for staff in the nursing home's hair salon to be knowledgeable about working with the hair of African American residents.

Some relatives of Jewish residents emphasized the importance of the Jewish sponsorship of the home for both residents and caregivers. A niece said that her aunt had not practiced Judaism until after her mother had died, but the Jewish sponsorship of the home made a difference to her. A resident's nephew said that the fact that it was a Jewish home had made the family feel better and that it would give his aunt comfort if she knew that the home was Jewish. A daughter said that being in a Jewish home had absolutely made a difference for her mother because of the Jewish activities, including holiday celebrations. The opportunity to speak Yiddish provided positive experiences for some residents. Religious services were also important to some of the residents and their relatives; the sister of a resident reported that the rabbi and the services added a new dimension to the resident's life. The son of another resident said that availability of religious services was important to his father and that his father's admission to a Jewish home provided an opportunity for the son to reconnect with his religion. Other relatives said that the Jewish affiliation of the home provided the residents and family caregivers with a sense of community or belonging, but some relatives did not believe that Jewish sponsorship had made any difference in the nursing home experience.

The experiences relating to ethnicity that Latina/o relatives most frequently discussed pertained to language. As noted previously, all of the Latina/o residents were born outside of the mainland United States, and although many had lived on the mainland for much of their adult lives, some had lived in ethnic communities, including the neighborhood in which the nursing home is located, and they had been able to continue using Spanish as their primary language within their families and communities. Additionally, some residents who had learned English as their second language had lost that knowledge because of short-term memory loss resulting from dementia, but their long-term memory retained the knowledge of Spanish learned early in life.

Although some of the Latina/o residents spoke English fluently, the limited English fluency of others led to difficulties when they were living on units that did not have Spanish-speaking staff and residents. Important language-related issues discussed by relatives included the need for Spanish-speaking staff on all shifts; the need to assign Spanish-speaking staff to

Spanish-speaking residents; and the importance of communication in Spanish in order to orient residents, help them retain their mental alertness, and provide quality care.

Service Provision

It's the best thing since popcorn!

—A resident's daughter, two years after her mother's admission

Asked whether they thought that anything should be changed at the nursing home, relatives and friends expressed satisfaction with most aspects of care, but some caregivers made specific suggestions for changes they would like. There was considerable overlap in issues raised by caregivers of African American and Afro-Caribbean, Jewish, and Latina/o residents. The issues mentioned most frequently were (1) the desire for more extensive discussion with staff at the time of admission and the need for opportunities to meet with staff at regular planned intervals; (2) care issues, including staff size and scheduling; and (3) staff attitudes, interpersonal skills, and confidentiality.

Several relatives said that they would like to have structured feedback from staff more frequently, preferably every three months, which was a shorter interval than the annual care plan meeting to which each resident and his or her sponsor (the primary contact person outside of the nursing home) were invited. At the time of this study, meetings were held more frequently only if the situation required. Related recommendations were that staff spend more time close to admission day meeting with the family to learn about the resident and also that occupational therapists orient residents after a move to a new room.

Regarding resident care, the relatives recommended better supervision of nursing assistants, as well as more volunteers, assignment of bilingual staff to residents who do not speak English, support groups for residents, and upgraded physician care. Provision of more "roaming" activities in which musicians and other recreational staff would provide entertainment in the rooms of residents with very limited mobility was also suggested. Specific suggestions regarding staff were that there be more staff on weekends, that fewer per diem workers be hired to work in the evenings, that floaters be better informed about the residents, and that weekend staff be as knowledgeable about residents and procedures as staff who worked weekdays.

Recommendations regarding staff attitudes, interpersonal skills, and confidentiality included greater compassion, patience, and emotional support, as well as the provision of counseling or training to help nursing assistants to be more sensitive to residents and their relatives and develop greater understanding of how to approach older persons. It was also recommended that staff be counseled not to discuss relatives with other residents' relatives and that staff understand that they should not speak to residents as if they were children, talk about them when they were present, or ask questions indirectly.

Evaluation of Services

I told my daughter, if I have a stroke I want to go there.
—A resident's daughter, six years after her mother's admission

The relatives and friends were asked how they felt about the nursing home now that their relative or friend had been living there for months or years. Fifty-nine of the caregivers gave completely positive responses, and only two gave a generally negative response, with one complaining about lack of care and respect and another saying, "I don't like it any more than when she came." While relatives and friends of the majority of African American and Afro-Caribbean, Jewish, and Latino residents responded positively, the comments of African American caregivers were overall the most positive. For example, one resident's daughter said, "I feel blessed for her to be here." The daughter of another resident said, "We love it. We like the staff, and she's being treated well." A granddaughter said that it was great, that "they have people from all walks of life and functioning." A friend said, "I like it. I play Bingo with them and come to sing along," and a resident's nephew said, "Well, I would say it's a class A act. It's a big operation." A resident's wife reported, "I think it's very good. I love their programs. People are friendly to him."

Some of the Jewish relatives had generally positive reactions, as illustrated by a grandson who said, "It's pretty good, and I like all the programs. It's a nice feeling," and a resident's wife who said, "It's a fine place. Considering the fact that he can't speak, it has gone well." A niece said, "The staff relates well to him" and that there was "attentive medical care." Positive responses by Latinas included a niece's comment that "I'm much more relaxed when I come here" and remarks by a daughter that "as time goes by, I'm beginning to feel much better and more peaceful." A resident's wife said, "I feel happy. My husband has very special care here," and a daughter said, "I am grateful because they've helped me. They're taking care of my mother." A son said that it was a good home, that "they've helped him out a lot."

Caregivers whose responses were not 100 percent positive generally identified only one or two areas of concern, and sometimes these were past issues that had been addressed effectively or that arose only occasionally.

Reflections on the Placement Decision

Sometimes I don't even want to think about it.
              —A resident's wife, two years after her husband's admission

I feel good about it. It was the only option I had.
              —A resident's niece, fourteen months after her aunt's admission

We think that it was the best decision. . . .We think that her health will not improve much.   —A resident's daughter, seven months after her mother's admission

The placement decision was extremely difficult for many of the residents and their families. When caregiving relatives and friends, most of whom had participated in the decision-making process, were asked months or years after the admission, "How do you feel about the decision now?" a large majority of the African American and Afro-Caribbean relatives and friends (twenty) and Latina/o relatives (eighteen) and about half of the relatives of Jewish residents (twelve) clearly indicated that placement had been the right thing to do or the best decision.

The positive attitudes of relatives of African American and Afro-Caribbean residents are apparent in such statements as the following: "It's the best place for her. If I end a conversation with her on a bad note, I don't have to worry through the night. Now I know she's taken care of." Another daughter said that she was comfortable with the decision, although she still wished that she had not had to do it. On the other hand, one daughter said that she didn't like it, that she preferred to have her mother at home, and another said that if there was something else she could do her mother wouldn't be in a nursing home, that if she lived near family they would take care of her mother in shifts.

The majority of Latina/o relatives were also positive about their decision. A daughter said, "I think that for the time it's the best decision I made," and a niece said, "I feel much better. I know I made the right decision." A daughter said, "it was the right decision to make; he's diabetic and had an amputation," while a wife whose husband had multiple medical problems said, "I feel better. I feel that I did something nice. He might have died if he was still with me," and a nephew said, "I'm very happy. She has good attention." In contrast, relatives who felt more negative about the decision included a daughter who thought relatives had placed her in a position in which "I have no choice. . . . I feel guilty" and a daughter who said that she still feels bad.

About half of the Jewish relatives clearly indicated that they believed they had done the right thing or made the right decision. A resident's sister said, "I think it was a wiser thing to do," and a niece said, "It was inevitable. She's gotten good care." On the other hand, many responses were negative or ambivalent, including a wife's response: "I'm alone. I'm alone in the house all the time. Sometimes I'm doubtful that I did the right thing. I still feel guilty at times." A son said that he felt a lot of guilt, that "as a child, there wasn't anything my mother wouldn't do for me." A sister said, "I'm not happy about it, but there's no other alternative." A daughter said that because her mother is lucid, sometimes it doesn't feel right, but she doesn't feel guilty, that she is a realist and has no regret about the decision that her mother and she made.

Long-Term Plans

I don't know. I live day to day. I pray to the Lord. How am I going to take care of her now? I have a heart condition.
> —A resident's daughter, three years after her mother's admission

I'll bring her home when she becomes more stable.
> —A resident's daughter, two years after her mother's admission

When asked whether they planned for their relative or friend to remain in the nursing home, the caregivers gave widely varying responses. Relatives of nineteen of the Jewish residents clearly indicated that they anticipated that their relative would remain in the nursing home, and this was also the expectation of relatives of fifteen Latina/o residents and the relatives and friends of thirteen African American and Afro-Caribbean residents. Some caregivers of Jewish and African American and Afro-Caribbean residents did not answer this question. For many caregivers, it was difficult to say that the resident would remain in the nursing home permanently, even when the caregivers were positive about the original placement decision.

Some of the caregivers expressed uncertainty or ambivalence about future plans, even when the plan at the time of the interview was that the resident would remain in the nursing home. For example, the son of a Jewish resident said that his plan was for his mother to remain in the nursing home because she would receive better care there, but the plan would change if there were positive results from an experimental drug that she would be taking in a research study. The daughter of an African American resident said that if she decided to move she would transfer her mother to a nursing home in another state so that her mother could live near her. Another daughter said that she sort of believed that her mother would remain in the nursing home but that the plan might change if the daughter could retire soon and get help and take her mother with her to her home. The son of a Latina resident said that his mother would remain in the nursing home if she stayed in her current condition, but "if she could walk again and go to the bathroom by herself, I'd take her home."

Other caregivers indicated that they did not know whether the resident would remain in the nursing home. Some Latina/o relatives said that they had no idea or that they didn't know. Other responses were "I don't know; we haven't made any decisions" and "If God helps me and gets me a home where he can have the help he has now, yes, I'll take him out, but not if it would not be better for him." Some of the Jewish caregivers responded, "I don't know; I'll see how it works out" and "Difficult to say; I don't know." Another relative said, "Sometimes I don't even want to think about it; I hope he will improve enough to go home." The relative of an African American resident said, "There's nothing else to be done right now."

The residents' move into the nursing home completed the transit stage, the transition that began with the decision-making process and continued through admission day. For the residents and their relatives and friends, contacts with staff during the admission process were generally positive, although a few relatives said that they would have liked some staff members to be more supportive. A few relatives were displeased with room and floor assignments, and these situations generally resulted from the home's financial need to assign new residents to the first available bed rather than delaying admission and the need to assign residents to floors where the appropriate level of care could be provided.

A broad range of emotions was in evidence at the time of admission among the caregiving residents and relatives in each of the ethnic and racial groups. Many of the Latina/o residents and relatives, in particular, experienced strong emotional reactions, including anger and depression, while others felt less distress. Some Jewish caregivers experienced depression, sadness, and guilt, while others did not. Some African American relatives were depressed, sad, or anxious, but did not indicate that they felt guilty, and the emotional responses of Jewish and African American and Afro-Caribbean residents were also quite varied.

Resettlement began when the admission process was completed, and over time caregivers and residents had the opportunity to see whether life in the nursing home was the same as or different from their expectations. Most experiences were positive, and many of the families were pleasantly surprised. Some, who had had negative expectations because of descriptions of nursing homes on television, discovered that this home was much better than what was portrayed.

Relatives and friends raised important issues regarding race and ethnicity and provision of services. Language was an issue for some of the relatives of Latina/o residents; the need to assign bilingual staff to provide services to residents who speak limited or no English is a critical component of that concern, since communication is essential in order to provide good services across all disciplines. Many Jewish residents regarded the Jewish sponsorship of the home or Jewish religious services as important, and some thought the opportunity to speak Yiddish with other residents was beneficial. African American and Afro-Caribbean relatives requested weekly Protestant services, as well as appropriate hair care. Some caregivers from each group cited the importance to residents of opportunities to eat foods that reflected their cultural heritage, and some relatives brought ethnic foods to the nursing home.

Because of the diversity of the older adult population in the United States, issues such as these are not unique to the residents of a single racial or ethnic background but are shared by residents of diverse racial and ethnic backgrounds in many nursing homes. For the best service to be provided, it is essential to be culturally sensitive in recruitment and training in professional and paraprofessional educational programs, in recruitment and training of nursing home staff, and in assigning residents and employees to nursing home floors.

Relatives and friends were satisfied with most aspects of care, but some changes were recommended. Fifty-nine caregivers evaluated services as completely positive, with the most positive responses overall coming from African American and Afro-Caribbean caregivers. Requests for change included more extensive discussions with staff members at the time of admission and more frequent meetings with staff, as well as suggestions about staff size and scheduling, staff attitudes, interpersonal skills, and confidentiality.

A large majority of African American and Latina/o relatives clearly indicated that they believed placement had been the right decision, while about half of the Jewish relatives expressed this belief. In view of these findings, it is interesting that nineteen of the relatives of Jewish residents, fifteen relatives and friends of Latina/o residents, and thirteen African American relatives anticipated that the resident would remain in the nursing home. Many variables influenced plans for the future, including caregivers' plans for their own lives and their perceptions of potential options for the residents.

The interviews also revealed that relatives and friends experienced similarities and differences in their caregiving responsibilities and in their emotional reactions after residents had moved to the nursing home compared to responsibilities before admission. Chapter 7 will address informal caregiving during the resettlement stage, and chapter 8 will address services provided by social workers and other staff in the nursing home.

7

CONTINUING TO CARE FOR RELATIVES IN THE NURSING HOME

It's a love thing. I don't see it as a responsibility. She was there for us. My mother worked, and she took care of us. . . . Deep within, I feel that I owe her something. You don't forget a bridge; she helped us over troubled waters.

> —A resident's niece, nine months after her aunt's admission

Now I have to help him. When I was young, he took care of me, so why can't I take a little time to take care of him?

> —A resident's son, four months after his father's admission

I'm still wondering. Why me?

> —A resident's daughter, two months after her father's admission

THIS CHAPTER DESCRIBES the caregiving tasks that relatives and friends had assumed since the residents' admission to the nursing home, their motivations for caregiving, and their emotional responses to caregiving responsibilities. I shall also discuss the issue of who the informal caregivers are who have helped the resident the most and why changes in caregivers occurred.

CAREGIVING TASKS

I feed her dinner when I go. I want to make sure that she gets a good meal.

> —A resident's daughter, six years after her mother's admission

Consistent with Dobrof's (1977) findings that in some families placement occurs because the family wants the best care and living situation for their relative, the relatives and friends in this study generally wanted the best for the residents and assumed responsibilities that would ensure the best quality of life for them as resettlement occurred. Some caregivers said that they assumed new and additional responsibilities after admission, others believed their responsibilities were similar, and some believed their responsibilities had diminished. The number of caregivers in the families varied greatly, as was true before placement. The three general types of responsibilities that caregivers assumed after admission were (1) formal responsibilities as sponsors, (2) informal monitoring of care provided by staff, and (3) tasks of a more personal nature.

Tasks related to formal responsibilities as a sponsor included making financial arrangements, completing required paperwork, and being the primary contact for consultation with administrative staff, clergy, and dietary, medical, nursing, occupational therapy, physical therapy, social work, and therapeutic recreation (activities) staff. This profile is consistent with the responsibilities of sponsors that Brody (1990) and Dobrof (1977) identified. For example, the niece of a Puerto Rican resident assumed responsibility for such tasks as having her aunt's bank account transferred after her admission. On an ongoing basis, relatives and friends interacted with staff regarding medical concerns, treatment needs, emergencies, and social and psychological issues related to cognitive loss, depression, behavior, mood, and changes in roommates. Sponsors were invited at least annually to a meeting with the interdisciplinary staff who were caring for their relative or friend so that they could participate in discussion of the resident's biopsychosocial functioning and care plan.

The second group of tasks pertained to informal monitoring of care provided by staff, including bathing, feeding, toileting, medications, and general care. The granddaughter of an African American resident said that she made sure that she was "on top of this place, a constant presence." A Jewish son said that he monitored his mother's health all the time. Some relatives said they monitored care in the nursing home more than they had monitored the care provided by home health aides before admission, and others said that their monitoring activity had diminished. Some families perceived the need for monitoring to be greater because care needs until admission had been minimal or nonexistent. Some relatives acted as advocates for the residents, discussing their concerns with staff.

The third group of tasks, of a more personal nature, included visiting, bringing ethnic foods and other food, feeding, managing finances, closing residents' homes after admission, serving as interpreters, providing emotional support, providing clothing, and washing residents' laundry at home. Some of these tasks were the same as the caregiving tasks mentioned in chapter 2, which were identified by Brody (1990) and documented by findings regarding tasks assumed in caregiving at home (Abel 1991; Brody 1990).

Visiting and attitudes about visiting varied greatly among African American and Afro-Caribbean, Latina/o, and Jewish caregivers. Health and geographic distance of relatives and friends affected their ability to visit, and proximity of the nursing home to caregivers' homes had been an important factor in the decisions of many families in choosing this facility.

Many of the relatives and friends visited as frequently as daily to every few weeks. Each of the twenty African American and Latina daughters whose mother was a resident visited at least every few weeks. A Puerto Rican daughter in a family in which caregiving for her mother was shared by several sisters said that someone visited daily. The wife of an African American resident said that she visited only occasionally because she was ninety-two, it was hard for her to travel, and her husband didn't recognize her. A Jewish resident's wife who believed that her life was "totally, totally different" since her husband's stroke said that she visited her husband all but a few days every week. A Jewish grandson said that he felt that he needed to see his grandmother more after she moved to the nursing home, that before her admission he used to visit her once a week but that no longer seemed enough.

For some relatives, visits had decreased after an initial adjustment period. The nephew of a Jewish resident said that he was more involved when his aunt was adjusting to the home and he had wanted to make sure that she was all right physically and secure and well taken care of, and he gradually decreased contact after she adjusted. The niece of another Jewish resident said that she visited at the beginning, but that many of the responsibilities for her aunt were taken care of by a conservator.

MOTIVATIONS FOR CAREGIVING
FOR NURSING HOME RESIDENTS

It's part of life. You do what you have to do.
> —A resident's brother, five years after his brother's admission

I always lived near her. My sister helped, too. The others were in Puerto Rico except for one who didn't help as much. My mother always needed help with things because she didn't speak English. I feel I have done my duty.
> —A resident's daughter, three years after her mother's admission

She took care of me, and we are taking care of her now. She took care of me when I couldn't help myself.

> —A resident's daughter, six years after her mother's admission

I want to help her. It's just how it has been since my childhood. I was always involved in my parents' decisions.

> —A resident's son, one year after his mother's admission

What motivates relatives and friends to continue as caregivers after nursing home admission takes place? The above quotations represent four types of motivating factors that were apparent in the responses of relatives and friends: (1) acceptance of caregiving as one of many responsibilities that a person must assume in life, (2) filial piety, (3) mutuality, and (4) caregiving as a result of intergenerationally shared discussion and decision making throughout the lifetime of the caregiver.

Some of the relatives held the attitude that caregiving is one of many responsibilities that must be accepted in life. Relatives of Jewish residents, especially those from the same generation as the residents, were the ones who most often expressed this belief. Glicksman (1990:14) noted: "Traditional Jewish values emphasize the importance of providing for the needs of the elderly and respect for the elderly. These two ideas, caring and respect, form the basis for all attitudes toward the aged." The biblical commandment to honor your father and mother has been important throughout Judaism, and the importance of caring for relatives was reinforced by life in host countries that would not take care of Jews (Ferster 2001). Therefore, Jewish families learned to accept responsibility for their own welfare and the welfare of other Jews; in Eastern Europe, this was carried out through the practice in large families of designating a family caregiver (Ferster 2001).

The expectation that individuals are to assume responsibility for assisting older relatives as a component of generally accepting responsibilities was evident in the statements of many Jewish caregivers. A resident's sister said, "Some people ask me why I visit her. I say, 'She's my sister.' We always accepted our responsibilities." A resident's brother said, "It's part of life. You do what you have to do," and the sister of another resident expressed a similar view when she said, "I don't find it difficult. We always had responsibility." The sister of a resident said, "What can I do? I have to accept it. I have one other sister in London. She doesn't fly, so I'm the only one." A resident's niece said, "There's no other choice."

A strong sense of commitment to following through with responsibilities because that is what one does was also evident in the responses of some African American caregivers. A daughter who was the only child said, "It's difficult, but you cope. . . . We do what we have to do." The sister of another resident said that she had been the person to do whatever needed to be done in the family; she had helped her mother, father, and sisters. For thirteen years she went to the city where her sister lived every weekend to provide assistance to her. She said she did not know why, but she quoted the "Golden Rule" as an explanation, saying, "Do unto others as you would have them do unto you."

The second motivator was filial piety. The literature suggests that filial piety, or filial responsibility or obligation, is a motivating factor in familial assistance to older relatives, particularly among Latino and Asian families (Connell and Gibson 1997; Finley, Roberts, and Banahan 1988; Garcia-Preto 1996; Selig, Tomlinson, and Hickey 1991). As Garcia-Preto (1996:151) has noted in her discussion of Latino families, "Perhaps the most significant value they share is the importance placed on family unity, welfare, and honor. The emphasis is on the group rather than on the individual. There is a deep sense of family commitment, obligation, and responsibility. The family guarantees protection and caretaking for life as long as the person stays within the system."

Facio (1997), who refers to her interpretation of filial responsibility as familism, has suggested that an alternative to the conceptualization of familism as an empirical or structural phenomenon is to regard it as an ideological force and identify its class, racial-ethnic, gender, and cultural origins. As noted by Kolb (2000:507), "Facio (1997:338) stated that the empirical phenomenon of familism, 'a manifestation of expected mutual aid and support,' may have changed even though the element of family unity remains; that is, unity may result from gender or age dynamics rather than familism or culture. She explored aspects of familism that are rooted in gender and suggested that patriarchy 'bonds women to motherhood and family caregiving roles,' which are important for maintaining the family (p. 339)."

The second quotation at the beginning of this section, ending with the statement "I feel I have done my duty," provides an example of attitudes of Latina/o family caregivers of Acacia residents related to filial piety. In contrast to the motivator of acceptance of caregiving as one of the many responsibilities to be assumed in life, statements by caregivers reflecting filial piety were more likely to reflect a sense of duty with regard to obligations of family members toward each other. While this quotation reflects comfort in accepting the responsibilities, some of the relatives were more ambivalent.

Latina daughters who were caregivers for their mothers were the participants who most frequently expressed filial piety. Filial responsibility was accompanied by the expectation that women would be the primary family caregivers, and the responses of four Latina daughters reflected particularly strong feelings of duty. These daughters expected similar behavior and attitudes from their siblings. Although all of the Latina daughters assisting their mothers indicated that other relatives had helped with caregiving before and/or after the placement, some of the daughters believed that brothers and sisters should share caregiving responsibilities and thought that they (the daughters) were doing more because they were women. Among Latina daughters caring for their mothers, negative feelings were most apparent when the daughters expected filial responsibility, had a strong belief in duty, and thought that the assistance provided by relatives was inadequate. The daughters' emotional responses to caregiving were also influenced by relationships among the adult children and residents' relationships with their other adult children.

Some of the Latinas described their work as caregivers in negative terms, and some communicated ambivalence regarding caregiving, while others described caregiving in positive terms. Ambivalence is consistent with Facio's (1997) research findings that older Chicanas are more accepting of the caregiving role when it is respected and not taken for granted. The ambivalence of a few of the daughters was reflected in some of their statements, including "I don't know why [I became the primary caregiver]. I'm the only sucker one. They called me to go to Puerto Rico to take care of her when she was sick. I wanted to return to this city, so I brought my mother and brother [here]." Another daughter said, "I don't want to do it, but they [my brothers] don't, so what am I going to do?"

The third motivator reflected in the responses was mutuality, reflected primarily by daughters of African American and Afro-Caribbean residents. Mutuality is a major concept in self-in-relation theory (Jordan 1991; Jordan et al. 1991; Turner 1997). This theoretical perspective emphasizes the importance of the mother-daughter relationship throughout life and suggests that both mothers and daughters learn to take care of their relationships and attend to each other's well-being and development (Surrey 1991).

Cultural variations within the self-in-relation model have been explored by Turner (1997), who suggested that the possibilities of connectedness for women of color may be increased within their cultures and with members of other minority cultures; she attributes this phenomenon to experiences of racial oppression and being bicultural in the United States. This view is consistent with the emphasis of Collins and other multiracial feminists on the influence of oppressive social structures on relationships of women of color (Baca-Zinn 1998; Baca-Zinn and Thornton-Dill 1997; Collins 1991, 1997; Facio 1997; Glenn 1992). In this study, two Latina daughters assisting their mothers also described motivations and emotions related to mutuality.

Among daughters for whom mutuality was a motivator, the tasks of monitoring care, visiting, and providing personal assistance appeared to be deliberate reciprocity for the physical care and protection that mothers had provided for them throughout their lives. These daughters' attitudes and expectations with regard to their caregiving roles as their mothers became older appeared to be related to the social construction throughout their lives of their roles as daughters of African American and Afro-Caribbean women in the United States. The third quotation at the beginning of this section reflects mutuality, as does the statement by another daughter who said, "I love doing it. We should because she did for us. It's a part of us. We take care of her." Acceptance of the responsibilities is also evident in another daughter's statement: "When I dream about home, it's my mother's home. . . . Your parents are a God-given, loving responsibility. It's a privilege."

Although many African American and Afro-Caribbean daughters appeared to be motivated by mutuality, some described the responsibilities as difficult. A daughter who had made decisions about medical interventions for her mother, including a feeding tube, said that she would rather not have had the responsibilities but accepted them because her mother would have accepted them. Another daughter said that being the primary caregiver was all right, but she would prefer to share the responsibilities with another caregiver.

The fourth motivator was the caregiver's expectation that caregiving should be provided because of the intergenerational relationship that had developed from shared discussion and decision making within the family throughout the caregiver's lifetime. As the fourth quotation at the beginning of this section indicates, for this son the desire to help his mother was a continuation of his desire to help since childhood and was influenced by his participation in decision making within his family throughout his life. Although he had accepted the fact that, because of deterioration in his mother's functioning, placement was the only workable option, he continued to feel guilty about the decision, saying, "As a child, there wasn't anything that my mother wouldn't do for me. . . . You feel guilty that you can't reciprocate." He would have liked for the outcome to be different, and although he anticipated that she would continue to live in the nursing home, he hoped that she would be helped enough in an experimental medication study that she would be able to leave.

This experience is consistent with the characteristics of the type of intergenerational relationship described as "tight-knit-helping" by Silverstein, Lawton, and Bengtson (1994) in their typology of relations between parents and adult children based on a research study on intergenerational linkages (Bengtson and Harootyan 1994). In "tight-knit-helping" relationships, parents and children score high on opportunity for meaningful interaction, based on geographic distance and frequency of contact; high on closeness, based on "feelings of *closeness* toward a parent or child, and [this] comprises emotional closeness and consensus, the perceived similarity of opinion with the member of the other generation"; and high on helping behavior, which is "informal assistance provided to and received from a parent or child" (Silverstein, Lawton, and Bengtson 1994:47).

This motivator resembles mutuality, but is different from mutuality as conceptualized in self-in-relation theory, in which it is linked to being female and to mother-daughter relationships. It is consistent with Antonucci and Akiyama's (1991) perspective in convoy theory of intergenerational relationships as bidirectional exchanges and expectations between children and parents that develop and change over time, contributing to intergenerational expectations within families regarding the care of older relatives. As indicated in chapter 2, convoy theory proposes that convoys of social support develop over the life course and, according to Antonucci and Akiyama (1991), the relationships generally enrich, fortify, and reassure but can also place individuals at risk and make them more vulnerable as aging occurs. In viewing the intergenerational relationship developed over a lifetime as a motivator for caregiving for relatives in this study, however, it is apparent that such relationships may develop within a dyad or a few dyads in a family in which there is not a large convoy of support.

EMOTIONAL RESPONSES TO CAREGIVING RESPONSIBILITIES

It's just fine. I feel like it's my responsibility. I don't know why I'm the only one who cares. —A resident's granddaughter, eight years after her grandmother's admission

Caregivers described a broad range of emotional responses to these responsibilities, including acceptance, anger, feelings of being trapped, fulfillment, guilt, resentment, sadness, satisfaction, stress, and weariness. Some viewed caregiving as a burden.

Responses of African American caregivers varied, but many indicated acceptance. A nephew said, "It's how things should be." A daughter also indicated her acceptance when she said, "It's a responsibility but not a responsibility; anything for her is okay." A nephew who had worked in nursing homes said, "My feelings are the same because they are related to geriatrics. Why should we abandon them?" Likewise, a resident's friend said, "It doesn't bother me; I look forward to getting up and doing what I need to do and coming here every day or every other day." In contrast, a granddaughter who had attempted to maintain her grandmother's apartment in case she returned home said that at first she was gung ho, but the responsibilities had worn her down. Several caregivers reflected emotional responses related to mutuality in their comments. A daughter said that assuming new responsibilities didn't bother her, that her mother was a good mother and she felt compassion for her.

Jewish caregivers reported varied responses as well, including acceptance, but one also mentioned feeling pressure to visit and help in other ways, and for another visiting felt like a burden. A niece who had little contact with her uncle before admission and for whom he was the third relative in rapid succession to move into a nursing home described it as "a bit of a burden." However, a husband who was in his nineties and visited frequently said that he wanted to assume the new responsibilities because he loved his wife, that it was not a burden.

Reactions among the Latina/o caregivers included acceptance based on filial piety, mutuality, or the belief that the responsibilities were very limited; resentment because of the lack of appreciation or assistance from other family members; feelings of being trapped; feelings of guilt when it was impossible to do everything that the caregiver expected of herself; and a feeling of additional pressure, but acceptance, described by a son who said, "It's a little bit more pressure because sometimes I have my things I need to do, but it's all right." A daughter who visited her mother several times each week said that she accepted the responsibilities and felt less responsibility compared to when her mother was at home and had home attendants. When a resident's son was asked about new responsibilities, he said, "I love to have them."

Some of the causes of emotional responses of caregivers in this study were among those identified in a study of thirty-one daughters who participated in focus groups in another study (Krause, Grant, and Long 1999).

The groups in the study identified eight major stressor themes: sense of responsibility, losses, role change, conflicting perceptions of parents' ability, realization of own vulnerabilities, facing the unknown, lack of family support, and lack of appropriate facility care (1999:353).

WHO HELPED THE MOST AND WHY WERE THERE CHANGES FROM ONE CAREGIVER TO ANOTHER?

Reflecting upon their experiences as caregivers, some participants reported that they were the person who had given the most assistance, while others said that sometimes other persons provided more assistance. A few participants, in spite of being the sponsor, had not provided the greatest amount of help at any time. Within the families, the individuals identified as providing the most help at various times were brothers, a cousin, daughters, daughters-in-law, friends, granddaughters, a grandson, a home attendant, husbands, neighbors, nephews, nieces, sisters, sisters-in-law, sons, sons-in-law, wives, and a former wife.

Availability was an important determinant of who would provide assistance, and in some families availability changed over time. Even when there was a large convoy of relatives and friends, not everyone was available to assist older family members, and sometimes no one in the family was involved. Sometimes interpersonal conflicts limited the number of caregivers who were willing to help. In one situation, the friend who had helped a resident the most said that the resident was a difficult person and that other people had not been able to take it, adding, "God has given me the strength to help her, and if I didn't help her no one would."

The caregivers as a group were quite diverse and were involved in assisting the residents for many different reasons. Although there is a female "ethic of care" (Doty, Jackson, and Crown 1998), in this study males participated very actively in caregiving. Some caregivers said that they were available to help because of stability in the long-term relationship with their partner, and sometimes partners shared caregiving responsibilities. Others said that they were the caregiver because they were single or did not have children.

Some of the caregivers for residents from each racial and ethnic group indicated that they had given the most help because no one else wanted the responsibility. In some of these situations, other relatives or formal caregivers had assisted previously, but arrangements changed after admission to the nursing home. In most of the families, relatives were supportive of the placement plan, but it is possible that some may have become less involved following admission because of general discomfort with a nursing home, with the resident's deteriorated functioning, or with issues pertaining to illness or death. Although Abel's (1991) study focused on caregiving prior to nursing home placement, she noted that for the daughters in her study the experience of providing care for their mothers engendered fears of aging and death, reflections on the changes in their lives, feelings of loss, and redefinition of their roles in relation to their mothers. Brody (1990) found that after placement some of the strains experienced by caregivers before placement continue while others emerge.

Some relatives became less able to provide assistance because of their own health problems. In one family, the resident's sister visited and continued to regard herself as the primary caregiver, but she had chronic medical problems and the person who spent a great deal of time visiting with the resident was a paid companion. In another family, a resident's younger sister-in-law began helping her sister and brother-in-law when her sister became ill, and she continued to help her brother-in-law even after her sister died and he had entered a nursing home. Illness of older relatives was one reason that a younger relative had taken over the caregiving responsibilities in some families, but sometimes members of the next generation had medical problems of their own that limited their availability as caregivers. A niece became involved when a resident's daughter became ill with cancer, for instance, and this niece considered the resident's former home attendant, who visited the resident in the nursing home, to be the person who helped the most.

In some families, a relative who helped the most had relocated or had moved the resident closer to where he or she lived. In one family, after the daughter and son-in-law who had helped the most moved to Florida, two other daughters who remained in the city became the most involved in assisting their mother. In another situation, a woman was receiving assistance in Puerto Rico from her sister-in-law and neighbors after a stroke, and a brother who lived in the city where Acacia was located went to Puerto Rico to help. His wife was ill, however, and it was difficult for him to remain in Puerto Rico, so after his sister fell he brought her to this city so that he could be closer to her to provide assistance.

In contrast to the popular belief that nursing home residents are abandoned by their families, it is apparent from this study that relatives and friends do remain involved after nursing home admission. All seventy-five residents had continued to receive assistance, in varying degrees, from at least one relative or friend since their admission, and this included residents who had been in the nursing home for many years. Considerable variation existed, however, in the tasks, motivations, emotional responses, and number and consistency of those caregivers.

Responsibilities assumed by caregivers of African American and Afro-Caribbean, Jewish, and Latina/o residents included (1) formal responsibilities as sponsors, (2) informal monitoring of care provided by staff, and (3) responsibilities of a more personal nature. Although participants in each group assumed responsibility in each of these areas, variations existed within each in terms of the assistance provided for each type of task.

Participation as sponsors included making financial arrangements, completing required paperwork, serving as primary contact for staff on the interdisciplinary team, and attending care planning meetings. Informal observation of staff care included monitoring bathing, toileting, feeding, medications, and general care, and caregivers assumed more, less, or a similar amount of monitoring responsibility than they had had before the admission. Tasks of a more personal nature included visiting, bringing ethnic and other food, feeding, managing finances, closing residents' homes after admission, monitoring health, serving as interpreters, providing emotional support, bringing clothing, and washing residents' laundry at home.

Motivation for providing assistance with these tasks resulted from (1) acceptance of caregiving as one of the many responsibilities in life, (2) filial piety, (3) mutuality, and (4) caregiving based on an intergenerational relationship developed through shared discussion and decision making within the family throughout the lifetime of the caregiver. Although the groups overlap to some extent, the first three motivators were expressed most often by relatives in a specific racial or ethnic group, lending support to the view that historical and/or cultural experiences of racial and ethnic groups can influence expectations about caregiving for at least some group members. The first motivator was reflected primarily in responses of relatives of Jewish residents and may be related to traditional Jewish values of respecting elderly persons and providing for their needs, as well as historical experiences of Jewish people in host countries in which they needed to take care of each other because the host country was not going to take care of them. Filial piety, or responsibility, was reflected primarily in the responses of Latina/o caregivers and was described by some as duty. Filial piety can be conceptualized as either a structural phenomenon or an ideological force rooted in class, racial-ethnic, gender, and cultural origins. The third motivator, mutuality, as conceptualized in self-in-relation theory, was reflected primarily in the responses of daughters of African American and Afro-Caribbean residents. Among the daughters for whom mutuality was a motivator, caregiving appeared to be deliberate reciprocity for the care that their mothers had provided to them throughout life in their roles as daughters of African American and Afro-Caribbean women experiencing racial oppression in the United States.

The fourth motivator may apply more broadly across racial and ethnic groups, and the family dynamics from which this originates resemble interaction in the "tight-knit-helping" family, which is described by Silverstein, Lawton, and Bengtson as scoring high on opportunity for meaningful interaction, high on closeness, and high on helping behavior in intergenerational relationships. It also resembles the intergenerational expectations described by Antonucci and Akiyama in convoy theory. Mutuality is also implied, but not as this concept is used in self-in-relation theory, which specifically emphasizes the importance of mother-daughter relationships.

Although all of the persons who were interviewed accepted caregiving responsibilities after the residents' admission, their emotional responses to caregiving were diverse, including acceptance, fulfillment, stress, anger, guilt, feelings of being trapped, resentment, satisfaction, weariness, and sadness. Some experienced caregiving tasks as a burden, while others did not. Variables influencing emotional responses included motivation for caregiving and availability of support.

Some persons who were interviewed had consistently been the primary caregiver, while others had not. Factors that influenced decisions about who would become a caregiver included availability of time, gender, health, and geographic proximity to the resident as well as family size and relationships of family members with each other and with the resident. Although there are cross-cultural expectations that females will be the family caregivers, this study confirms that some males have a strong commitment to assisting older relatives and continue providing assistance following a relative's admission to the nursing home.

In some families, the primary caregivers had changed over time, for such reasons as declining health or geographic relocation of a caregiver or resident. Other causes may have been the caregivers' discomfort with aspects of nursing homes and the residents, with their relative's increased physical or cognitive deterioration, or general concerns about illness and death.

8

WHO HELPS RESIDENTS
AND THEIR RELATIVES?

Everybody has been nice. A Spanish-speaking nursing assistant has been very nice to her. This has made a real difference. She gives her a lot of attention.

—A resident's niece, one year after her aunt's admission

For me, the daughters' support group has been helpful, especially regarding specific issues having to do with care.

—A resident's daughter, three years after her mother's admission

The physical therapy and occupational therapy departments were great.

—A resident's niece, one year after her aunt's admission

IN THE PREVIOUS CHAPTERS, this book has focused primarily on the experiences of the nursing home residents and their caregiving relatives and friends and has included much less information about the formal network of paid caregivers who provided a great deal of assistance before and after admission to Acacia Nursing Home. This chapter shifts attention to the paraprofessionals and professionals, reporting information about staff assistance that the relatives and friends considered "especially helpful," structural impediments to nursing home service delivery, national workforce issues in nursing home care, alternatives to nursing home placement, and implications of this study's findings for provision of ethnically and racially sensitive services.

QUALITY CARE: ESPECIALLY HELPFUL STAFF

Some of the evening attendants are beautiful.

—A resident's granddaughter, eight months after her grandmother's admission

The head nurse on the early shift is very nice. He thinks a lot of her. He goes to her if there is a problem, and she helps him out.

—A resident's wife, one year after her husband's admission

The student project was especially helpful. He loves when people ask him about the family. —A resident's daughter, two years after her father's admission

The "especially helpful" behaviors described by participants were most often actions above and beyond basic job responsibilities and generally involved empathic service delivery rather than additional time on the job. Compassion. A smile. A kind, caring, tone of voice. Respect rather than infantilization. Human connection rather than robotic service delivery. These were approaches to providing services in which relationships, events, emotions, and difficulties in residents' and caregivers' lives were acknowledged and validated.

The work of certified nursing assistants (CNAs) and orderlies is difficult and demanding, but many relatives who responded to this question, particularly Latina/o relatives, described great kindness on the part of CNAs and orderlies. Latina/o caregivers may have especially valued such behavior because of the cultural values of *familismo* and *personalismo* (Moreno 2002). A daughter said that certain staff understood how to toilet her mother the best and that one of the nursing assistants was very tender. Another daughter said that an orderly who worked during the day was especially helpful, bringing her mother juice, and another said that many of the nursing assistants were nice to her mother and showed her respect, that they changed her colostomy bag often. Another daughter said that some of the orderlies had been especially sensitive to her father. A son said that a nursing assistant who worked in the evenings was very sensitive and took good care of his mother. A granddaughter said that an orderly was very nice to her father, that the orderly "takes it personally." A daughter said that sometimes orderlies, nursing assistants, and nurses noticed that she was down and were supportive.

Relatives of some of the Jewish residents also identified orderlies and nursing assistants as having done something especially helpful. A niece said, "One time when my aunt was starting to act up, an orderly took the time to talk with her and helped to calm her and put her situation into perspective for her." A son said that the nursing assistants for his mother during both the day and the evening shifts are especially helpful and caring. Another son also referred to the nursing assistants as especially helpful.

A few relatives and friends of African American and Afro-Caribbean residents also praised nursing assistants. A daughter believed that a nursing assistant who had taken care of her mother for three years had been especially helpful, and a nephew said that when there was a problem regarding his aunt's television a nursing assistant explained the problem to the nephew and cared about what had happened.

Others whom the caregivers and families mentioned as being especially helpful included accounting staff, recreation therapists, doctors, nurses, occupational therapists, social workers, and a social work student. In addition to commending social work services provided to individuals, some relatives of residents considered a support group for residents' daughters that was begun by a social work graduate student and continued by a staff social worker for many years to be especially helpful, as well as a project carried out by social work graduate students that provided opportunities for residents to reminisce about their lives.

IMPEDIMENTS TO NURSING HOME SERVICE DELIVERY

This section provides a brief overview of information about external and internal systemic factors that affect the provision of nursing home care throughout the United States. In general, Acacia Nursing Home offers good-quality services, provided by a large complement of staff from many disciplines, as well as a capable corps of volunteers, but some of the relatives of residents had been concerned before admission about the quality of care in nursing homes, and some of those concerns remained after admission. Although members of the staff had the benefits of union membership and the advantages that accrue from working in a home that prides itself on its national reputation for quality care, the challenges resulting from workload size and the inherent difficulty of the work were significant.

Scandals in other nursing homes in the past have resulted in closer monitoring by federal and state government agencies and private organizations in order to improve the quality of care, but several authors have reported mixed findings from the 1970s, 1980s, and 1990s regarding quality of care. Throughout the nursing home industry certain systemic issues exist that impede staff implementation of the kinds of actions that earn the commendation "especially helpful" from informal caregivers of residents.

Many anthropological and sociological studies have documented contemporary systemic issues and positive and negative aspects of life in nursing homes (Diamond 1992; Gubrium 1997; Savishinsky 1991; Shield 1988; Tisdale 1987; Vladeck 1980). In general, these studies did not address issues related to the race and ethnicity of the residents, although some studies have addressed issues related to race, ethnicity, and gender with regard to staff. The major issues addressed in the literature are lack of quality care due to the profit motive, lack of staff training and adequate pay, difficulties in measuring or controlling quality of care, instability of the medical and psychological makeup of nursing home residents and nursing homes, presence or absence of bureaucratization, inability of residents to repay staff, the home-versus-hospital dichotomy, the medicalized model of nursing home care, commodification of residents and staff, estrangement of residents from control over their lives, existence of different "worlds" and "places" of administrative and floor staff and residents, the shift of nursing homes on a continuum toward the acute care hospital and away from home, loss of personal care floors and the addition of short-term subacute care, Medicare's prospective payment system, and the influence of multiple market factors.

Bruce C. Vladeck raised many concerns about nursing home care in 1980 when he published *Unloving Care: The Nursing Home Tragedy*, reporting the results of his extensive study of public policies that influence the development of nursing homes in the United States. Addressing quality of care, Vladeck wrote:

> High quality nursing home care consists of the maintenance of a clean and pleasant environment, in which the food is good, that there is plenty to do, assistance is readily given with dressing and bathing, people are nice to each other and respect each other's privacy and personal dignity, and good medical and nursing services are provided to those who need them. This may seem like a simple set of requirements, but in practice, it is not.
>
> Few nursing homes are of high quality by these standards. It is inherently difficult to provide intimate personal services to severely disabled, often hostile or disoriented, physically and emotionally frail people, especially when most of those providing services are untrained and poorly paid and when the facility's operator is trying to make a profit on $25 a day, at least 10 percent of which goes to mortgage payments. Only the most exceptional institutions provide really good food. The customary practice of medical care is potentially inimicable to personal privacy and dignity. And ensuring that everyone is kept busy too easily shades into regimentation and manipulation.
>
> If it is difficult to provide high quality care, it is more difficult still to measure or control it. Moreover, both the medical and psychological makeup of nursing home residents and nursing homes are highly

unstable. What is appropriate care for a resident one week may be scandalously inadequate and inhumane the next, if her condition deteriorates, or demeaning and patronizing, if it improves. A first-rate nursing home can become a terrible one in the course of weeks if it loses a good nursing director and a good cook.

Finally, most nursing homes are small, informal, nonhierarchical, and nonbureaucratic—characteristics that are otherwise desirable but that make regulation substantially more difficult. The large number of separate facilities further exacerbates this problem, since the greater the number of sites to be inspected, the greater the workload of the inspection system.   (1980:148–149)

Although care has generally improved in many nursing homes, some authors reporting findings from more recent studies have expressed concern about more extensive bureaucratization, particularly in hierarchical structures in which there is little contact between managers and floor workers and residents.

In 1988 anthropologist Renee Rose Shield published *Uneasy Endings: Daily Life in an American Nursing Home*, which she described as an anthropological study of a "good" nursing home in the Northeast, at the same time expressing concerns about some issues, including the lack of opportunities for residents to provide repayment and the home-versus-hospital dichotomy. She identified the following salient issues:

> The study of the Franklin Nursing Home offers a mixed view. A well-thought-of nursing home, Franklin offers many good services. Many of the recipients express satisfaction at being there and actively chose to be admitted, and many staff members demonstrate sensitive and caring qualities. On the other hand, this institution shares with others the problems of insensitive and ambivalent treatment of the aged. . . .
>
> The ability to give, receive, and repay seems to be so basic to human social life that it is often the crucial mark of personhood. The inability to repay, on the other hand, is often a criterion of not being a "real" person. In the United States being a recipient is ambivalently perceived both as a right and as a stigma. Status as a recipient is linked to being dependent, and being dependent in turn is associated with nonresponsible, nonautonomous, childlike status.
>
> The home-versus-hospital dichotomy that underlies the lifeways of the institution, reflecting divisions in staff ideologies and preventing

staff and resident cohesion, connects the ideas of reciprocity and liminality. . . . Notions associated with the home idea have to do with
community, purpose, connectedness, and comfort. Members of a
well-functioning home work together, assert their allegiance to one
another, and rearticulate in new forms and contexts how they are
meaningful to one another. In the hospital, on the other hand, patients
are sick, receive care by staff members, and comply with staff orders.
Patients need not communicate with one another; their primary relationship is with the doctor and the other staff members ministering to
them individually. Further, they need not be active in getting well.
Home principles in this analogy therefore translate into community
and reciprocity, and hospital principles correspond to isolation, pas-
sivity, and nonreciprocity. In the nursing home there is evidence of
community and reciprocity when home factors come to the fore.
These are the times when staff members and residents act like friends,
when residents demonstrate support for one another by helping out,
and when residents work together in physical therapy to improve
their condition.   (1988:214–215)

In her book, Shield (1988:21–22) introduced the concept of liminality with
Victor Turner's (1967) meaning of "all kinds of people and situations that
are defined as neither in one category of social identity or another." However, Turner stressed "the positive aspects of liminality and used the term
communitas to describe the togetherness that initiates in a rite of passage often shared with one another," and Shield argued that nursing home residents
are undergoing a rite of passage and make a transition between the old role
and the new role (liminality) but that their liminality is not marked by *communitas*. In her opinion, the community fails to support the nursing home
and the residents adequately. McLean and Perkinson (1995:127) have noted that "the regimentation imposed by the bureaucratic organization, the interpretation and response of the staff to bureaucratic constraints, and the
even less visible pressures that influence the way staff interprets and structures its approach to caregiving" may be unanticipated conditions that have
a dramatic impact on new residents.

The medicalized model of nursing home care and its influence on the development of nursing home culture and the issues inherent in this approach
were addressed by anthropologists Henderson and Vesperi as editors of *The
Culture of Long Term Care: Nursing Home Ethnography* (1995). In their view, "in
our desperate attempts to solve the so-called problem of old-age disability,

we look to the medical model for answers. We reformulate human existential dilemmas as clinical problems. Perhaps nowhere is this cultural tension between medicine and morals played out more elaborately than in the American nursing home" (1995:ix).

Henderson (1995) reported anthropological findings from an ethnographic study in which he gathered information as a participant observer at "Pecan Grove Manor," a ninety-bed skilled nursing facility in a southern midwestern state, while working as a certified nursing assistant (CNA) and observing CNA work:

> Overall, the administration and staff placed a great emphasis on the quality of care for the patients of Pecan Grove Manor. The emphasis on caring for the patients was sincere, as many personal gestures of true care and concern were shown to most patients, both publicly and behind the scenes. There was, however, a failure to see the larger picture of patient life through the eyes of the patients. "Basic (i.e., physical) care" was the gold standard for measuring quality of life. Still, there were regulations that mandated psychosocial care in the form of "activities." Consequently, activities were undertaken, but they were of the simplest kind and were accompanied by the attitude that a mere charade was sufficient. It was in the psychosocial care domain that there was the greatest staff blindness to what quality of life in long term care should and could be.
>
> The product of this organizational culture was that patients with chronic, incurable disease lived their remaining days in a system based on acute care hospital models. Psychosocial care was a footnote grudgingly delivered in muted forms. Although the patients' mood and spirit were amenable to nurturing and improvement, the physical care model was master.   (Henderson 1995:38–39)

Bureaucratization of nursing home care and its effects on staff and residents is a key theme in sociologist Timothy Diamond's ethnography, *Making Gray Gold: Narratives of Nursing Home Care* (1992), which was based on participation observation while he was employed in nursing homes as a CNA. Diamond (1992:172) pointed out that nursing homes are arenas of caregiving, but they are also bureaucratic organizations founded on specific relations of power. In the context of being made into a business, caregiving becomes something that is bought and sold. This process involves both ownership and the construction of goods and services that can be measured and priced so that a bottom line can be brought into being. It entails the enforcement of certain power relations and means of production so that those who live in nursing homes and those who tend to them can be made into commodities and cost-accountable units.

Diamond (1992:172–173) illustrated this commodification of residents and staff by noting that nursing assistants were repeatedly assigned to tasks for specific "beds," such as beds 201 to 216, with "beds" referring to persons, which "makes persons into things." He noted that *efficiency* was a favorite word, "as it is in all businesses, . . . tied to the labor force and the abilities of the administration to produce the product with the fewest employees, within a specific calculus of labor costs" (1992:175). CNA staff had been reduced, and the demands on the remaining CNAs were greater than they could meet. While staff labored under these conditions, Diamond (1992:179) observed residents "expressing specific desires [toileting, ambulation, appetizing food] while encased within a system of control that precluded them from satisfying their own needs." According to Diamond (1992:179), residents became "estranged from authority over their own food, cleaning, and medications, as needs, how they were to be met and which ones would remain unmet, became externally defined." He (1992:180) suggested that the creation of concepts, scales, measures, and resulting work practices contained in documents, such as residents' use of diapers rather than toileting, are produced by professionals and managers removed from these experiences and are perceived to be "indicators of good health care business."

Sociologist Jaber F. Gubrium originally published his study of the social organization of care in one nursing home, *Living and Dying at Murray Manor*, in 1975, and a new edition was published in 1997. In the new edition, Gubrium (xxii) returned to his 1975 perspective of the nursing home as a place with "several different organizations in practice," or "worlds," "separate and distinct from the outside and yet whole and reasonable from within." Furthermore, he suggested that the "reasonableness of separate worlds" was secured by both perspective and "place," with top staff working in their offices and in meetings and floor staff spending most of their time on patient and resident floors, coming into contact primarily with the residents and each other (1997:xxiii).

Consistent with Diamond's description of power relations in nursing homes in which he worked, Gubrium (1997:xxii) wrote that in Murray Manor "regular references by the floor staff to 'them,' meaning the administrative staff, conveyed a sense of being outside of important channels of decision-making affecting their work. Comments such as 'we' know what we want, meaning what patients desire as opposed to what staff considers is best for 'them,' signaled a shared reasonableness among equals that outsiders couldn't, or perhaps wouldn't, understand." He (1997:xxii–xxiii) continues: "My sense was that administrators ('top staff'), as well intentioned as I actually found them to be, worked in a separate world from the floor staff. What the top staff saw as good and efficient caregiving, floor staff could consider 'just getting the job done.' The residents and patients, too, lived in their respective worlds which separated them in terms of what they took for granted as reasonable expectations from the floor staff. What a resident felt was time well spent chatting with a friendly nurse's aide could, from the aide's point of view, be time away from other duties." Similarly, Holstein (2001:93) noted, in a review of Diamond's *Making Gray Gold*: "Aides respond to patient needs; when they can, they build relationships, but they always know that unquantifiable activity does not count."

In 1997, Gubrium identified changes in long-term care that had occurred in the years since he had conducted his fieldwork at Murray Manor. He noted that the position of nursing homes on the continuum of care across which people in the United States are treated and otherwise cared for had shifted since the 1970s so that it had become closer to the acute care hospital end of the continuum than to the nursing home end. The trend in nursing homes had been toward increased specialization so that some have "formally designated subacute care units for postacute hospital care, requiring physician supervision and skilled nursing services combined with physiological monitoring on a continuous basis" (Gubrium 1997:xv). Murray Manor and most other nursing homes in the early 1970s divided the services into skilled and intermediate nursing care and personal care and did not have special care units. However, by 1997, some nursing homes had formed special care units (SCUs) for persons with Alzheimer's disease and other dementias, rehabilitation, or hospice care. By the time of the interviews on which *Caring for Our Elders* is based, the nursing home in the study had had a short-term rehabilitation unit for several years. In 1996, of the total of 1.8 million beds in the 16,840 nursing homes in the United States, 73,400 beds were in Alzheimer's special care units and 28,500 were in rehabilitation and/or subacute special care units (Rhoades and Krauss 1999).

In her ethnography, *Harvest Moon: Portrait of a Nursing Home* (1987), Sallie Tisdale wrote about a nursing home with 100 "beds," of which 60 were allocated for intermediate care for persons who were neither acutely ill nor dying but who could not live independently and whose stay at Harvest

Moon was of indeterminate length. She suggested that "a few generations ago these patients would have been cared for in the back bedroom of the farmhouse, ministered to by women of various ages and degrees of relation, until their invalid state finally killed them" (1987:10).

Gubrium (1997:xvi) and others have explained changes by identifying market forces that have contributed to change. Market forces were apparent in the development of a subacute care unit in the mid-1990s at Acacia Nursing Home. Contributing factors included concerns regarding potential reductions in Medicaid reimbursements, anticipated revenues from subacute care, and the interest of managed-care companies in saving money by reducing the length of patient stays in acute care hospitals and transferring patients to nursing homes for subacute care at a rate that was less costly than acute care hospital rates.

Subacute care in nursing homes was evident in the results of my nationwide survey of trends in social service delivery in nursing homes, conducted in 1997–1998 (Kolb 1998). Respondents in 37 of the 298 homes that returned the questionnaire said that their home had beds that were allocated specifically for subacute care, and 65 percent of these homes were owned by corporate chains. When asked how many beds were currently occupied by persons for whom managed-care companies were paying the cost, 56 homes responded that they had occupied beds for which managed care was paying at the time of the survey. The number of residents whose stay was paid for by managed care was 7 or fewer in 43 of these homes, and some respondents did not know whether there were managed-care patients in their home.

According to Gubrium (1997), market forces influencing changes in nursing homes included development in the early 1980s of Medicare's prospective payment system for hospitals, which provided standard payments to hospitals for groups of diagnoses, or diagnosis-related groups (DRGs). With this system, Medicare pays hospitals a fixed amount based on the diagnosis, a change from the previous practice of reimbursing hospitals for charges for each of the services provided. Hospitals responded by discharging patients "quicker and sicker" (Gubrium 1997:xvi), and this practice led to nursing homes' admitting patients who were sicker than ever (Estes and Swan 1993). Gubrium (1997:xvi) predicted that "combined with the increasing specialization of care in nursing homes, the result will be that the distinction between these facilities and hospitals in the future will be even more blurred." Tisdale (1987:96) suggested that "the idea that large for-profit corporations would voluntarily lose money on half of a commodity out of kindness is truly a wonder. The DRG system has created instead distasteful incentive programs that encourage physicians to discharge patients when their money runs out, regardless of the patients' conditions." At Acacia Nursing Home, residents were occasionally admitted from hospitals when they still needed acute care hospitalization; these individuals were quickly returned to the hospital for the necessary additional treatment.

Addressing the implications of the Medicare reimbursement system for Harvest Moon residents and other nursing home residents with Medicare, Tisdale (1987:85), wrote:

> The Medicare system is full of backwaters and impediments, described in long columns of entangled lingo and code words. The regulations hold two themes especially dear: first, that these rules and explanations are lucid and clear, that there is nothing vague, no area for disagreement. The second theme of Medicare, strengthened a few years ago as the main thrust of Medicare's brave new future, is that every person is the same. This is a blank and blanket assumption: that every patient with the same diagnosis will suffer and recover in the same way and in the *same period of time*. It is a very strange assumption, utterly insupportable, and contrary to the most basic understanding of health and illness.

In order for nursing homes to receive Medicare reimbursement, strict documentation is required pertaining to services reimbursable for a very limited group of DRG categories. Tisdale (1987:92) wrote:

> The nurses must document not only the care they give, but the reason for providing skilled nursing care, every day, every shift. If a person is considered a skilled-care patient because they have a nasogastric feeding tube and will, it is hoped, learn to eat again, then every shift the nurses must note the placement of the NG tube, the number of times it is used, whether or not oral feedings are offered, and how both oral and tube feedings are tolerated. She must also write in her notes—and she writes one for each of her fifteen to twenty patients every day—about the person's activities, their mental state, their routine, their bowel and bladder, the condition of their skin, whether they have worn restraints, whether they show signs of any medical problems, such as a fever, in what ways they are limited in caring for themselves, if any teaching was done and how it was received, and whether the goals in the care plan are being met.

Nurses on each of the floors in Acacia Nursing Home, on which *Caring for Our Elders* is based, were responsible for care and documentation for an even larger number of residents, from twenty-five to thirty-eight per floor.

The development of assisted-living facilities and home health services is another market force that has contributed to change (Gubrium 1997:xvi). Assisted-living facilities that offer meals and help with activities of daily living (ADLs) provide the kind of personal care that Murray Manor did in the 1970s, but now these services are usually centered in residential settings other than nursing homes. At Acacia Nursing Home, some floors had previously been designated "health related," in addition to the "skilled nursing" floors, but by the mid-1990s all floors in the nursing home were designated skilled nursing floors except for the "rehab," or rehabilitation floor, and the subacute floors, which were added at this time.

NATIONAL WORKFORCE ISSUES IN NURSING HOME CARE

Acacia Nursing Home generally had well-trained and adequate numbers of staff persons, but workers across disciplines felt the pressure of a great many tasks to accomplish during their workday. Workforce issues in the care of older adults have been raised in several studies, and grave concerns have been expressed about the potential to recruit enough workers in the twenty-first century to meet the national need (Diamond 1992; Henderson 1995; Johnson and Grant 1985; Savishinsky 1991; Shield 1988; Stone 2001; Stone and Wiener 2001; Tisdale 1987). The spring 2001 issue of *Generations*, published by the American Society on Aging, was devoted entirely to workforce issues and addressed a wide variety of subjects, including sociodemographic change, policy, financing, cultural competence, technology, direct-care health care workers, social workers, geriatric nurse practitioners, allied health workers, and geriatric medicine. A 2001 report by Robyn Stone and Joshua Wiener, *Who Will Care for Us? Addressing the Long-Term Care Workforce Crisis*, explored issues pertaining to the paraprofessional workforce.

These studies and reports have generally focused on two broad workforce issues: the working conditions of service providers and the adequacy of the workforce relative to the number of workers needed in the past, present, and future. These issues are interrelated because the anticipated working conditions in geriatric services are likely to influence decision making about entering the workforce, and the number of workers will affect working conditions for employees in the workforce, especially CNAs and orderlies, the front-line workers in nursing homes.

The increasing number of people in the United States who live to old age, the larger numbers of women who work outside the home, and higher divorce rates have contributed to the increased need for formal caregiving. In the twenty-first century, changing demographics, including aging of the baby boom generation, increasing numbers of minority elderly, and better-educated and higher-income elders will also influence the need for long-term care and long-term-care staffing (Alecxih 2001:7–9). Demographic shifts in the availability of informal support will include an increase in the proportion of married older persons through 2030, and although married people are less likely to use long-term care, fewer women with children will be available as a potential source of support because childlessness among women age 40 to 44 began to increase with the cohort of women born during World War II (1940–1944) (Alecxih 2001:10–11). Therefore, Alecxih has suggested, more women may need to rely on spouses, friends, and paid caregivers for support.

A Workforce Crisis: Nursing Assistants

Concern about the anticipated lack of workers in long-term care, including staff for nursing homes and home care, has focused particularly on paraprofessional workers and the essential services that they provide. Stone (2001:49) has described their work as follows:

> The paraprofessional long-term-care workforce—nursing assistants (NAs) and homecare aides, personal care workers and personal care attendants—forms the centerpiece of the formal long-term-care system. These so-called frontline workers provide hands-on care to millions of elderly and younger people with chronic illness and disabilities in settings ranging from the nursing home to assisted living and other residential care options to private homes. The care is intimate, personal, and both physically and emotionally challenging. Because of their ongoing, daily contact with the care recipient and the relationships that often develop between the worker and the client, these front-line workers are frequently the "eyes and ears" of the care system. In addition to helping with activities of daily living such as bathing, dressing, using the toilet, and eating, these workers provide the "high touch" that is essential to quality of life as well as quality of care for chronically disabled individuals.

This description is consistent with the roles and responsibilities assumed by the CNAs and orderlies at Acacia Nursing Home and the "high touch" provided to residents and their relatives described earlier in this chapter. For example, the evening attendants that a resident's granddaughter described as "beautiful" impressed her very positively during the eight months since her grandmother's admission to the nursing home, despite the difficulties of their work. Residents are important to many CNAs. In a heartwarming publication, *Speaking from Experience*, the forty-two CNAs at Cobble Hill Health Center in Brooklyn shared their insights; they mentioned interacting with residents, being appreciated, working with other staff, getting satisfaction from helping others, and growing in the job as some of the rewards of their work.

The U.S. Bureau of Labor Statistics (2000) has predicted that between 1998 and 2008, 325,000 more nursing assistants and 433,000 more personal care and home health aide jobs will become available, but it is unlikely that the workforce will be sufficient to fill all of these positions. Stone and Wiener (2001:9) note the high turnover rate of 45 percent to 105 percent cited for CNAs in nursing homes, as well as the lower, but variable, turnover rates among home care workers. Lower unemployment rates and opportunities for higher-paying jobs with better working conditions for women contribute to a shortage of home care workers. Salaries tend to be only a little higher than minimum wage—the 1998 national median hourly wage for nursing assistants in nursing and personal care facilities was $7.50, and paraprofessional workers tend to lack health insurance (Stone and Wiener 2001:12).

Stone and Wiener (2001:11–12) provide an overview of the demographic composition of the long-term-care workforce in the United States:

As is true with informal caregivers, most frontline long-term care workers are women. According to national data on this work force from 1987 through 1989 (Crown 1994), an estimated 93 percent of NAs and home care workers were female. A 1995 survey of home care workers reported that 96 percent of those employed by agencies—and 100 percent of the self-employed—were female (Leon and Franco 1998). Crown (1994) estimated that almost 7 out of 10 [frontline long-term care] workers were white; 27 percent of the NAs and 29 percent of home care aides were black. More recent data from the BLS [Bureau of Labor Statistics] (1999) indicate that 35 percent of NAs are black and 10 percent are Hispanic. There is also significant geographic variation in the racial profile of frontline workers.

A recent study of home care workers participating in California's IHSS program found that 32 percent of the agency workers and 41 percent of the independent providers (including paid family caregivers) were white (Benjamin et al. 2000). Forty-five percent of the agency workers and 30 percent of the independent providers were Hispanic; comparable estimates for black workers were 15 percent and 20 percent, respectively.

Important gender, race, and ethnicity issues are evident in the low pay, nonexistent or minimal benefits, and poor working conditions of the great many women and members of racial and ethnic minority groups who make up a very large proportion of the frontline workforce that provides the most care to older adults who need formal assistance. These policies are damaging to quality of life and reduce opportunities, as Diamond learned when he worked as a CNA. He wrote: "The very concepts of job and wage versus unemployment and poverty that I had brought with me began to break down. What had been clear distinctions in my mind, and in the sociology literature, began to mesh together in real life. Everyday talk continued to center on not having enough money for rent or transportation or children's necessities. Full-time work meant earning less than the cost of subsistence; it did not alleviate poverty" (1992:44–45).

Initiatives developed to address problems with recruitment and retention have included creating "wage pass throughs" (a process by which "a state designates some portion of a public long-term care program's reimbursement increase to be used specifically to increase wages and/or benefits for frontline workers"). These include increasing workers' fringe benefits; building career ladders with additional job levels, new training requirements, new pools of workers; and establishing public authorities to address concerns of independent workers and consumers (Stone and Wiener 2001:5–6).

Stone and Wiener described several innovative interventions undertaken by providers and frontline workers, including the "Pioneer Homes" provider initiative, which attempts to change nursing home culture by trying to "link the facility to the outside world and create a community," and the Wellspring model, a consortium of eleven nursing homes whose management is committed to quality improvement through "a three-pronged approach [which] includes intensive clinical training, periodic analysis of outcomes data to monitor quality, and a management change/job redesign effort, in which nursing assistants become essential members of care teams and are empowered to make certain decisions." Initiatives by long-term care workers themselves include the Service Employees International Union (SEIU) and the National Network of Career Nursing Assistants.

Social Workers

The need for social work with older adults will increase, but there is a severe shortage of social workers with the commitment and competence to work exclusively with older adults (Barusch, Greene, and Connelly 1990; Peterson 1990; Rosen and Persky 1997; Rosen and Zlotnik 2001). Social work's biopsychosocial perspective and emphasis on culturally sensitive services are important contributions to services for older adults. Rosen and Zlotnik (2001:69) have accurately described the unique contributions of social work in the field of aging:

> Social work is unique among health and mental health professions because its practitioners are trained to consider the physical, mental, and social aspects of a person. Social work offers a comprehensive approach to human development that is essential in the provision of services to older adults and their families. The changes associated with aging have significant effects on an older adult's quality of life and on the need for supportive services. The comprehensive view of human needs that social work offers makes the social worker a key member of interdisciplinary service-delivery teams. . . . Moreover, social work professionals, particularly those working in healthcare and social services, will be increasingly involved with a diverse population of older clients and their families (Peterson and Wendt, 1990; Damon-Rodriguez and Lubben, 1997). The emphasis in social work education on cultural competence is well suited to this growing diversity.

An area of critical importance in recruitment and training of geriatric social workers is recruitment of persons from diverse ethnic, racial, and socioeconomic backgrounds into social work educational programs at the baccalaureate and master's levels, as well as hiring experienced social workers from diverse backgrounds to work with older adults and their families. Candidates include persons in non–social work employment who provide services to older adults and enjoy working with them and who have the ability and desire to pursue higher education and become social workers. Second, for the best social work practice with older adults and their families from diverse backgrounds, it is essential to provide training in many venues at many levels—undergraduate, graduate, certificate programs, inservice, and professional conferences—that increases understanding and acceptance of cultural differences in attitudes and values regarding family and the roles of older adults within families and communities, expectations about dependence and care in old age, and differences in attitudes and experiences regarding institutional care. Social workers can become "culture mediators" who interpret "ethnic influences that motivate clients . . . to others [in interdisciplinary teams in health care settings] to ensure appropriate treatment" (Fandetti and Goldmeier 1988:171).

Until recently, initiatives to increase visibility, interest, and education in geriatric social work have been very limited, although efforts by organizations including the Alzheimer's and Related Disorders Association, the Fan Fox and Leslie R. Samuels Foundation, and the Veterans Administration have provided some training or funding in this area. Training has been available through some gerontology centers at universities that also have social work programs, including the Brookdale Center on Aging of Hunter College, City University of New York.

In 1998 the John A. Hartford Foundation of New York began to fund major social work projects that include a field practicum initiative, a faculty scholars program, a doctoral fellows program, the Strengthening Aging and Gerontology Education in Social Work (SAGE-SW) project of the Council on Social Work Education, and Geriatric Enrichment in Social Work Education, which includes curriculum enrichment projects in baccalaureate, master's, and combined baccalaureate and master's programs throughout the United States.

Nurses

This country is currently experiencing a shortage of nurses at all training levels, including geriatric nurse practitioners, because of such factors as "aging and incipient retirement of the baby boom generation; increasing career options for women; and the persistent perception of nursing as a trade rather than a profession" (Fulmer, Flaherty, and Medley 2001:72–73). Nursing homes, also referred to as "skilled nursing facilities," provide twenty-four-hour service by licensed nurses to meet the total nursing needs for each patient (Johnson and Grant 1985). The general need to recruit nurses to work in the field of geriatric nursing is great, including recruitment for employment in nursing homes, a setting where skilled nursing care is an essential service if a facility is to be considered a nursing home.

One approach to addressing the nursing shortage has been to recruit nurses from foreign countries; some of the nurses at Acacia Nursing Home were from other countries. Stone and Wiener (2001:21) noted: "In the health and long-term care sector, [immigration] rules have been loosened to address the severe nursing shortage in hospitals, and, to a lesser extent, in nursing homes." While this strategy has been advantageous in meeting staffing needs in nursing homes, as well as adding ethnic and racial diversity among staff, it is a policy that contributes to the "brain drain" from less-developed countries. Timothy Diamond addressed the macro-level international implications of this policy when he described a mealtime conversation with nurses from the Philippines, Nigeria, South Korea, and Haiti. He reflected that "nursing homes expand as an industry within a world economic labor force. Sitting around that table in this seemingly autonomous nursing home, with its rustic, restful-sounding name, were nurses working in a multinational corporate context, in which the health care system of advanced capitalist societies depends on the work of Third World women" (1992:41–42). Laina, a nurse with whom Diamond worked, described her career path from the Philippines to employment in a nursing home in the United States:

> "There were something like fifty nursing schools in Manila when I was there, and just about everybody was going to work in another country when they graduated, most in the States." Toward the end of her five-year training program, which awarded her a bachelor's degree in nursing, she and her fellow students signed contracts with an agency in Manila. The contract specified the particular nursing home corporation for which she would work, the exact city, and the starting date. "Some company has to petition you to come to work," she explained. "But there's always jobs." (Diamond 1992:40)

Strategies to address the lack of trained geriatric nurses have also included training initiatives sponsored by such organizations as the Consortium of New York Education Centers, which is based at the New York University School of Nursing. Its mission supports the need for cultural competence in geriatric health care, as it states that the consortium attempts to "improve and expand geriatric healthcare particularly for low-income, multi-ethnic, and underserved older adults throughout New York State [and to] provide interdisciplinary, cutting-edge training courses on issues, treatments. and service delivery models to a broad range of healthcare professionals and academic leaders" (Consortium of New York Geriatric Education Centers 2001:7). The John A. Hartford Foundation has funded major initiatives in geriatric nursing, including the John A. Hartford Foundation Institute for Geriatric Nursing and the Nurses Improving Care for Health System Elders (NICHE) training program at New York University.

Physicians

At Acacia Nursing Home, physicians were assigned to specific floors in order to achieve consistency in medical care. Although nursing homes are required to provide medical services, too few physicians in the United States are trained in geriatric medicine. Blanchette and Flynn have presented compelling evidence of the lack of geriatricians and the need to address the lack of adequate training in geriatrics in medical schools. They note that many "problems emerge after the age of 75, when prevention, risk-factor modification, atypical presentation of disease, multiple chronic conditions, and intervention run counter to traditional principles of internal medicine used in caring for older adults. Social isolation, emotional vulnerability, and poverty complicate these problems and make interdisciplinary care mandatory for optimal treatment. Older patients react differently to medications, and it is common for them to be taking multiple drugs ordered by multiple physicians" (2001:80). They also note that in older adults illnesses may be misdiagnosed, overlooked, or dismissed, and as a result, preventable nursing home admissions take place, needless suffering occurs, and health care systemic costs escalate. Studies show that mistakes occur in medicine and other disciplines because of cultural misunderstanding when a service provider lacks adequate knowledge of the patient's and family's cultural beliefs and values regarding sickness and treatment, as well as of the patient's language (McGoldrick, Giordano, and Pearce 1996).

Compensation and career mobility are important issues in the field of geriatric medicine, and Blanchette and Flynn (2001:83) report that compensation issues are exacerbated by the Medicare system of physician reimbursement, which expects that reimbursement in a caseload will average out over time, failing to consider the complexity and additional time for patient care that a geriatric practice demands.

As in its support for social work and nursing, the John A. Hartford Foundation has funded initiatives to support the development of geriatric medicine. These programs have included the Paul Beeson Physician Faculty Scholars in Aging Research Program, which invests in promising junior faculty with the goal of increasing the number of physician-scientists who will become leaders in the field; a project to integrate geriatrics into subspecialties of internal medicine; and a project to increase geriatrics in the surgical and medical specialties (John A. Hartford Foundation 2001).

Allied Health Care Providers

Residents in the nursing home also received the services of allied health care providers, including occupational therapists, physical therapists, and therapeutic recreation (activity) specialists. The work of service providers in allied health fields includes interventions related to functional ability and elements of life that "beyond survival, define satisfying existence" (Bonder 2001; Csikczmentihayli 1975). Bonder (2001:77) and Diener, Suh, and Oishi (1997) have advised that it is important for training curricula to include material on assessment and interventions that support "quality of life, as opposed to a state of absolute health," especially for frail older adults.

Bonder has noted that cultural competence is an essential aspect of service in all of the allied health fields. At Acacia it was important for recreation therapists to be familiar with cultural knowledge, history, and traditions of the residents in their therapeutic interventions with them. The therapists' ability to facilitate activities that evoked residents' memories and emotions regarding past experiences embedded in culture was especially important for those with advanced dementia, as well as for those whose degree of cognitive functioning was more intact, and required understanding of residents' past experiences. While the standards for practice in allied health fields do mention cultural competence, they do not identify the necessary skills to achieve that competence. Recruitment of people from diverse racial and ethnic backgrounds to serve in the allied health professions also needs improvement (Bonder 2001:78).

In recent years, job opportunities in allied health fields have diminished because of cost-containment measures and the growth of managed care, and salaries have stagnated, but new employment opportunities for work with frail older adults in low vision, technology consulting, and other nontraditional service settings are developing (Bonder 2001).

ALTERNATIVES TO NURSING HOME PLACEMENT

In many families, particularly those in which strong cultural prohibitions against nursing home placement operate, the idea of admission to a nursing home is anathema. Yet structural lag exists, and often families can find no adequate alternatives to institutionalization after illnesses develop. An extensive array of informal and formal assistance addressed the needs of many of the older adults in this study before their admission to Acacia. Home health care workers, primarily from publicly funded agencies, provided between four and twenty-four hours of assistance daily; private home care services also existed, but their high cost generally precluded their being used. Ultimately, such factors as the time required for caregiving, the physical and emotional demands of caregiving, lack of an adequate combination of informal and formal services, environmental circumstances like the lack of an elevator in the building, and concern for the safety of the older adult resulted in nursing home placement even if relatives were strongly committed to care in the community. The available informal and formal services finally became inadequate for continued community residence.

It is apparent that there are African American and Afro-Caribbean, Jewish, and Latina/o relatives of families of various sizes who want to help older family members, need assistance from formal providers to do so, and find that the available services are not adequate to meet the needs. Particularly since many families need to continue working outside of the home, formal assistance is critical to the success of families' being able to maintain relatives at home.

Lacayo states that as a nation we must direct policy toward comprehensive community-based care and alternatives to institutionalization as a more balanced approach to meeting the health needs of minority elderly and other older Americans. In her view, alternatives are particularly important for the Hispanic community, for whom nursing homes (*asilos*) are often a dreaded place of last resort, used only when no other health care alternative remains. Lacayo suggests that a comprehensive continuum of long-term care services should be available, including in-home and community-based care for the "at-risk" aged and disabled population (Lacayo 1993:231).

The structural changes proposed by Lacayo constitute goals that would be beneficial in addressing the needs of many individuals. First, she advocates that the federal Medicaid match be increased. She also advises that states complete assessments of people who are at risk of institutionalization because of the lack of community resources, provide more resources for these individuals, limit reimbursement rates for community services so that they do not exceed those of nursing homes, and "coordinate long-term care and community-based services with similar services provided under other legislation" (Lacayo 1993:231–232).

Likewise, Angel and Angel (1997:138) point out that even good nursing homes are not like the older person's home, that "the desire to stay home is strong, and that a familiar environment is central to an older person's well-being. . . . Much of the justification for community-based care, therefore, is based on its potential for enhancing the quality of an older person's life." They believe that the larger world may seem hostile and foreign to an older adult who belongs to a minority group, and thus his or her familiar environment becomes even more important. They define community-based long-term care as "any formally provided package of services that allows a person to stay at home, or as close to home as possible."

Angel and Angel identify characteristics of an enriching and fulfilling community care system:

> First, it must offer the older individual and his family a wide variety of options in living arrangements, from group housing to remaining at home. Second, it must offer family members a wide variety of options in the extent of their personal involvement, so that they are not faced with either an impossible caregiving burden or the necessity of institutionalizing an aging parent. Third, it must integrate the older person into the community to the greatest degree possible, so that he or she is not isolated. Fourth, it must be designed in every way to complement rather than to replace the family and the informal support network. Fifth, and finally, it must provide these services at a cost that is no greater, or only marginally greater, than that of placing the person in a nursing home. (137)

They also say that the design of a community-based system must consider race and ethnicity, as well as life experiences and personality, and that formal systems should work with preexisting institutions in the community, such as the church.

Angel and Angel give some attention to problems that may arise if community-based services are expanded. Concerns focus primarily on the potential for greatly increased governmental expenses. The need for services exceeds the availability, and if more community services are offered, the demand for them may be great. Some believe that if government-sponsored services are expanded, they might replace informal care, at potentially staggering costs. Community-based care has generally not cost less than nursing home care, although a few innovative programs show promise of addressing this issue successfully. If community-based services are expanded in the future, it is possible that eligibility for participation may have to be based on need, which could result in the stigma and political vulnerability that already generally exist in programs for poor persons (Angel and Angel 1997). Furthermore, sometimes older adults live with their families out of necessity, and Angel and Angel warn that as programs are developed, planners should not penalize large families with whom an older relative is living by assuming that resources should go only to older adults with no other source of support. They point out that this practice could favor the non-Hispanic white and middle-class elderly and be disadvantageous to black and Hispanic older adults, who tend to have more children and whose children tend to remain in the same geographic area as their parents; the result might be a two-tiered system stratified by ethnicity and race.

Because assistance from community-based programs has not generally been less expensive than nursing home care, the rationale for these programs is that many older adults and their families, including some of the families described here, would like for older adults to remain in the community and that normal community life provides richer experiences than the nursing home environment (Angel and Angel 1997). Many older adults do not need assistance, but for those who do, an adequate combination of informal and formal community services may be preferable to nursing home care and often provides satisfying and fulfilling life experiences.

While it is true that community-based programs provide important options for older adults and their families, some older adults have a very limited support system or have a support system but lack assistance for coordination of needed services; for such people a nursing home can reduce isolation and provide opportunities for more reliable services and fulfilling experiences. Some people find that though their health care needs can be addressed adequately in the community, opportunities for social interaction, support, and mental stimulation may be much greater in a good nursing home.

Available community services include those funded federally through the Older Americans Act (OAA), among them information and referral, case management, transportation, nutrition, legal assistance, and home care. OAA funds are allocated to local area agencies on aging throughout the United States on a contract basis. Only a small proportion of older adults use the services funded through OAA, and the usage of specific services differs by ethnic group. Puerto Ricans are more likely than other Latinas/os and the general population of older people to use home health aides, including visiting nurse services, transportation, and homemaker services (Angel and Angel

1997; Hing and Bloom 1990; Westat 1989). Some of these services are also available in programs with state or local funding, such as senior citizens centers, programs for older adults living in areas that are considered Naturally Occurring Retirement Communities (NORC), and long-term home health care programs, including the "nursing home without walls," or Lombardi, program in New York State.

Other programs include respite care, adult day care, and housing programs, such as "board and care" and subsidized housing through federal agencies like the Department of Housing and Urban Development (HUD) and Section 8. Adult day care programs, as well as long-term home health care programs, provide Medicaid-reimbursable services, but the cost of participation for older adults who are not Medicaid eligible precludes the participation of many people who need the services. Funding for subsidized apartment buildings for older adults and for subsidized rents in other buildings has not kept up with the great need for housing assistance.

Although a broad range of community-based services provide vital assistance that helps many older adults to continue to live in their homes after they need assistance, few cost-effective service program models involve informal and formal caregivers in community care that provides long-term care services that are adequate to enable frail older adults to remain in the community when they otherwise would need to live in a nursing home. One such program, however, is On Lok Senior Health Services in San Francisco's Chinatown. This program, which has attracted close scrutiny, has successfully addressed the major structural gap in services for frail elderly persons and recognizes the importance of participants' traditional ethnic values, family support, and desire to remain in their own community. If a similar program had been available in Acacia's city, it most likely would have successfully met the biopsychosocial needs of most of the residents and their families in this study well enough to provide an alternative to nursing home placement, while also supporting cultural values and expectations regarding familial participation, food, and other needs. More programs developed on the On Lok model, tailored to racial and ethnic variations in values and customs, community size, politics, power structures, and other community characteristics, would reduce the current structural lag.

Angel and Angel (1997:150, 153) have written that On Lok

makes maximum use of local community resources and the informal network and has demonstrated that, with sufficient help, even the most seriously impaired older individuals can be kept in the community. On

Lok is a paradigm of the sort of coordinated program that combines the formal and informal support system to make the best use of family, community, and health care system resources and hence to improve the quality of life for the older person and his or her family. On Lok Senior Health Services is a consolidated model of community-based long-term care that integrates the full range of primary, acute, and long-term care services for frail elderly people eligible for nursing home care . . . in a familiar environment and in a manner appropriate for its ethnically homogeneous clientele.

Angel and Angel advise that "intensive interaction between program designers and the community is the key element" in efforts to replicate this model.

On Lok provides comprehensive services, reimbursable by Medicare, Medicaid, and private insurance, to older adults who would otherwise need to live in a nursing home. It emphasizes community residence and involvement, utilizes a multidisciplinary assessment team that consolidates service delivery, and requires that financial risk be assumed by care providers (Angel and Angel 1997:151). Services are provided through adult day care centers, clinics, and housing facilities, and costs are controlled through preventive health screening, emphasis on psychosocial well-being, maximizing functional capacity, and "providing low-cost services in the least restrictive settings, including the participant's own home," as well as billing at the higher per capita Medicaid rate because of the high-risk nature of the population served (Ansak 1990; Angel and Angel 1997:151–152).

ETHNICALLY AND RACIALLY SENSITIVE SERVICES

Previous life experiences shaped the values and attitudes of Acacia residents and their informal and formal caregivers regarding individual behavior and relationships, including their expectations about care of older family members who need assistance. Socialization plays an important role in the development of expectations in the ethnic and racial groups within which a person is reared, and socialization varies among and within groups. It is apparent that attitudes, values, and behavior are both shared and different within and among groups and that many variables besides experiences related to race and ethnicity influence attitudes, values, and behavior.

To understand individuals' premigration and departure, transit, and resettlement experiences in the nursing home placement process, service providers must be aware of the historical experiences and cultural values related to ethnicity and race that influence attitudes and expectations about care of older adults who need assistance. This awareness includes understanding the experiences of immigrants, migrants, and refugees from the perspective of the stage-of-migration process (Drachman and Ryan 1991; Drachman 1992).

"Cultural Competence" and Service Provision

Formal service providers came into contact with the Acacia residents and their relatives and friends in community agencies, in private doctors' offices, in hospital clinics and inpatient floors, in residents' homes, in the nursing homes in which residents had lived previously, in the admissions office at the nursing home, and on the nursing home floors and activity areas. They worked as homemakers, home health aides, home attendants, certified nursing assistants, social workers, nurses, geriatric nurse practitioners, physicians in various specialties (including psychiatry), nutritionists, therapeutic recreation specialists, occupational therapists, physical therapists, and students in professional training programs.

This study provides a great many examples of why service providers need to understand cultural values and behavioral expectations learned through socialization and reinforced within communities and why they need to consider these factors in engagement, assessment, diagnosis, planning, intervention, and evaluation of processes and outcomes in work with clients/patients and their relatives and friends. It is apparent that the capacity to "shift the center," "putting at the center of our thinking the experiences of groups who have formerly been excluded" (Andersen and Collins 2001:14), is essential for service providers who want to assist with the empowerment of members of groups that have been marginalized.

According to Andersen and Collins, shifting the center leads to reconstruction of knowledge, which helps members of both dominant and subordinate groups understand the partiality of their own perspective, create better social analysis and policy, and provide a reminder that knowledge provides a necessary orientation to the world. They believe that "inclusive thinking shifts our thinking from the white, male-centered forms of thinking that have characterized much of Western thought, helping us better understand the intersections of race, class, and gender in the experiences of all groups, including those with privilege and power" (Andersen and Collins 2001:15). If service providers shift the center, they are more likely to understand the experiences of their client or patient from that individual's own perspective, and validate *all* of the experiences of the older adult and his or her family and friends. In addition to the influences of race, class, gender, and socioeconomic status, age, citizenship status, disabilities and abilities, history of familial and other relationships, history of immigration/migration, personality, and sexual orientation contribute to the uniqueness of individuals who need assistance. These other influences can also require shifting the center in order to understand the experiences of older adults and their caregivers.

This approach is consistent with Bonder, Martin, and Miracle's (2001:36) concept of culture as "culture emergent," which they base on "the notion of culture as expressed through individual behavior reflecting the multiple influences that shape human experience: culture emerges in interaction of transient circumstances and traditional patterns of behavior." They suggest that the idea of culture emergent results in five suppositions that are useful in professional practice. The first is that people learn culture that is transmitted from one generation to another; Bonder, Martin, and Miracle point out that "older adults have had a great deal of time to learn cultural values and beliefs from those groups with which they have had contact." Second, "culture is localized. Culture is created through specific interactions with specific individuals. Each person draws meaningful elements from these interactions and shares them with some but not all individuals within society. . . . Interactions in multiple social settings may provide multiple contexts for learning culture." Third, "culture is patterned. Patterns emerge from the repetition of specific samples of behavior and talk. Repeated patterns establish the normal and customary explanations that structure social interactions. Elders often rely on such patterns to support their performance. Habit and ritual may be central to their lives." Fourth, "culture is evaluative. Values are a central component of culture and are reflected in individual behaviors. Values reflect shared beliefs that facilitate the social interaction without which society would not be possible. However, individuals continuously evaluate societal values in terms of personal relevance. The value systems of elders reflect the interactions they have had over a lifetime." The fifth supposition is that "culture has continuity, with change. In general, cultural identity is stable, but one's cultural knowledge changes over the life course as one encounters new objects, situations, and ideas in the personal environment. These experiences shape a unique person. Across society, many individuals may experience the forces for change almost simultaneously and respond in similar, although not identical, ways.

Although the popular perception is that elders change little, the reality is that they must be masters of adaptability to adapt to the alterations in their physical, cognitive, and social environments. Their values and patterns give them a structure within which to manage these changes."

Addressing the need for a practical approach for health care providers to practice cultural competency, Bonder, Martin, and Miracle (2001:37–38) propose an ethnographic approach as an alternative to limiting oneself to the fact-centered approach, "which provides information about the health beliefs and behavior of particular ethnic groups," or the attitude-centered approach, which emphasizes the "importance of valuing all cultures." Acknowledging that some factual knowledge is vital and that it is important to grant the centrality of culture and encourage positive attitudes, they also propose that an ethnographic approach to cultural competence based on anthropological methods provides a strategy of "learning how to ask" (Bonder, Martin, and Miracle 2001; Briggs 1986). They propose that this approach enables service providers to achieve the three skills proposed by Sue (2000) as necessary for engaging in effective intercultural intervention: scientific-mindedness, dynamic sizing skills (recognition of when to generalize or individualize in interaction with clients), and culture-specific expertise.

Describing the ethnographic approach, Bonder and colleagues (2001:39) recommend:

Clinicians must ask their clients for help in understanding the value systems from which they come. And they should make sure their clients feel that any cultural differences they may have with the clinician are respected and acknowledged during the therapy process (Sleek, 1998). The clinician needs to gather information effectively, identify goals, and provide interventions that reflect the client's cultural as well as medical needs. In intercultural interaction, gathering and using information to ensure outcomes identified by the client as positive are particularly challenging.

When working with a frail elder, part of the assessment process is determined by the clinician's professional background. This background might dictate, for example, questions about social networks, physical mobility, and auditory deficits. The clearest possible picture of the client's "culture emergent" is vital information from the perspective of every profession. However, it is not possible to "see" or focus on every aspect of a situation or environment. Thus, the clinician must assess cultural aspects of daily life and the construction of the current illness or disability. How does culture affect the client's social networks, mobility requirements, demands on auditory abilities, and general sense of well-being? What beliefs does the individual have about his or her current health situation and the place of older adults in the society? And, perhaps most important, what matters to the person? Johnson and his colleagues (1995) indicate that practitioners must (1) know how culture influences illness behavior; (2) determine when cultural differences are important; (3) elicit explanatory models for symptoms; and (4) recognize common ethnic explanation models.

It is not just the individual's culture that is important, but also the social structure of the culture. For frail elders, family and social environments significantly affect outcomes, and both are affected by culture.

Bonder and her colleagues emphasize the value of qualitative interviewing as an approach to obtaining culturally relevant information. Their conceptualization of qualitative interviewing is consistent with the attitudes and approach of the Acacia study in interviewing caregivers. In their view, "The essential element is careful listening for meaning not only in content but also in tone, word choice, body language, and other contextual clues. Effective qualitative interviewing requires empathy, sensitivity, humor, and sincerity. The interviewer must recognize his or her own biases and beliefs. . . . Such strategies as clarifying your purpose and asking permission can establish an atmosphere of respect. Requests for clarification and elaboration demonstrate interest, and careful observation can provide clues to proper behavior" (Bonder 2001:40–41).

While valuing the unique combination of experiences and characteristics within each individual, service providers must also understand the effects of widespread macro-level social changes on diverse groups of people. The need of older adults and their families for services is a "public issue" (Mills 1959). Social changes such as increased life expectancy, more women working outside of the home, and higher divorce rates contribute to greater challenges for many persons who want to provide assistance to older relatives so that they can remain at home. A very broad cross-section of families in the United States, racially, ethnically, and socioeconomically, are caught up in these challenges. The experiences described in this book attest to the effects of these issues on some African American and Afro-Caribbean, Jewish, and Latino families. These realities contribute to situations in which the decision is made to place an older relative in a nursing home, even if that solution is in firm opposition to the cultural beliefs of the older adult, his or her family, and their community. Alternatives to nursing homes are limited, and service providers must be aware of structural lag and work to develop more options that can provide culturally sensitive and cost-effective long-term-care services that are comprehensive enough to meet the needs of very frail persons and their informal caregivers.

MAJOR CONCEPTS IN CARING FOR OUR ELDERS

This study has identified several concepts related to race and ethnicity, based on the experiences of the residents of Acacia Nursing Home and their relatives and friends:

1. *Values, attitudes, and experiences related to race and ethnicity influence attitudes about aging and dependency, as well as tasks performed by caregivers, motivation for caregiving, and emotional responses to caregiving before and after nursing home placement.*

Service providers must avoid racial and ethnic stereotyping and strive instead to accept and understand variations in experiences within and among racial and ethnic groups. Attitudes of clients/patients and service providers vary regarding informal and formal care of older adults who need assistance, nursing home placement, dependency, interpretations of the etiology and social significance of dementia and other illnesses, and caregiving. Service providers need to practice empathy, professional objectivity, and willingness to examine their own values and preconceived ideas and learn from their clients/patients.

It is important to understand the history and cultural traditions of members of racial and ethnic groups, including the premigration and departure, transit, and resettlement experiences of immigrants and migrants. Traditional values, including expectations about roles and care later in life, may be reinforced within families and ethnic communities long after immigration or migration has occurred.

Service providers also need to remember that institutional and personal discrimination directed toward members of racial and ethnic minority groups has resulted in a disproportionate number of poor people in many of these groups, and therefore people from these groups may be less able to afford expensive home care and accessible housing that could enable families to further delay nursing home placement or avoid it entirely. While some members of minority groups do not have access to expensive community services, they may at times also be subjected to discriminatory practices in referrals to nursing homes and acceptance into homes on the basis of race and/or ethnicity, although this did not happen to the Acacia residents.

2. *Some relatives and friends within each group are willing to provide assistance in the community despite great difficulties in doing so but will pursue nursing home placement when the safety of the older adult becomes jeopardized because the available assistance is inadequate.*

Service providers in the community and in nursing homes need to remember that even within families and communities that have a strong cultural prohibition against nursing home placement, placement may be chosen when no other available alternative ensures the safety of the older adult. Older adults and their relatives and friends considering placement may need a great deal of information and support from service providers, especially if strong cultural prohibitions against placement exist and if this is the first time that they have participated in the placement process. Nursing home placement was the last resort for most of the caregivers in each group who participated in this study, and decision making, admission day, and the adjustment period were very difficult for most participants.

3. *Deterioration in an older relative's functioning may mean loss of valuable support to younger family members, including assistance with child care, particularly in cultures that traditionally value intergenerational assistance and in which family members live in close proximity with each other.*

Service providers should be aware of the potential loss of assistance to the family, especially if illness resulting in placement has a sudden onset, as is often the case with strokes. Family members need opportunities to discuss their emotional reactions to this loss, as well as access to information about alternative resources. Residents need opportunities to discuss roles that they have played in the family and the community and their emotional reactions to these losses.

4. *In the majority of families within each group, the resident who participated in this study was the first person who had lived in a nursing home, reflecting the changing nature of aging experiences within diverse groups over time.*

Social changes including increased life expectancy, higher rates of female employment outside of the home, and higher divorce rates affected the lives of some caregivers in each group and contributed directly or indirectly to the placement decision. While some residents and caregivers understood and accepted the changes within their families, others appeared to find it more difficult to do so and to accept the need for nursing home admission. Residents and their caregivers need opportunities to talk about changes in roles and responsibilities within their families and the consequences of these changes.

5. Location was the most important factor in each group for choosing this nursing home, and a large number of Latina/o relatives lived in the neighborhood.

Since a great many families do not want to "abandon" their relatives who are in nursing homes, service providers need to work with them to arrange admission to homes that are conveniently located for visiting and other caregiving. Many caregivers are elderly themselves and find traveling farther distances especially difficult.

6. Paternalistic, rather than autonomous, decision making about nursing home placement may be likely to occur in families in which older adults have retained traditional values that are antithetical to nursing home placement, but younger family members are confronted with the difficulties of caregiving in a modern industrialized society.

Service providers need to be mindful that it may be very difficult for members of both the older and the younger generations to accept the younger generation's taking control of the decision-making process, in an apparent intergenerational "role reversal" that is contrary to their traditional cultural expectations. Any assessment of family interaction and planning of interventions to assist and empower each involved family member must keep this dynamic in mind.

7. Residents, relatives, and friends may know very little about nursing homes and the placement process at the time that they decide to explore that option, and what knowledge they do have may be based on negative accounts in the media.

Families or friendship groups that face decisions about nursing home placement for the first time are in a unique and uncomfortable position. The professional health care providers—social workers in community agencies, physicians, hospital social workers, and nursing home admissions staff—play an important role at this juncture in providing adequate information that can empower the decision makers to make the very best choices. Access to good information and to emotional support can help families to avoid unnecessary difficulties.

8. Relatives and friends involved with the placement process, particularly if strong cultural prohibitions operate against nursing home placement and/or this is the first placement experience for the family, need to meet with a nursing home staff member at the time of admission or shortly thereafter to discuss the placement process, changes that have taken place in the life of the resident and family/friends, and emotional reactions to these experiences.

Nursing home personnel should ask the residents and their relatives and friends whether they prefer to be interviewed together or separately. Some topics that they want to discuss may contradict stereotypes held by the service provider. For example, a Latina caregiver may view caregiving as burdensome because of lack of support from family, but the service provider's stereotype may be that Latina/o families are large and include many available caregivers and that Latinas are glad to sacrifice themselves and help older relatives at all times. The staff member who is best prepared to have this discussion will most likely be the social worker, since social workers are trained to approach persons from a biopsychosocial perspective. Staff members should remember that the placement process can affect caregivers and residents on many levels—biological, psychological, and social.

9. Following admission, residents may have needs related to aspects of their race, ethnicity, or religion. It is important that staff address these needs in order to provide the best quality of life for all residents.

Many of the Jewish relatives and residents valued the fact that Acacia was a Jewish home and especially appreciated the religious services, clergy, and use of Yiddish. However, a great many nursing home residents live in homes where cultural practices that are familiar to them are absent. In these situations the families and staff should explore the feasibility of institutional changes. At Acacia, for example, some Latina/o residents spoke little or no English, and family caregivers and friends expressed concern when no staff member on the resident's floor spoke English or when Spanish-speaking nursing assistants worked on the floor but were not assigned to the non-English-speaking residents. The issue of communication is critical, for medical conditions may be overlooked or misdiagnosed if resident and service provider cannot understand each other. Relatives considered language important in orienting residents, retention of mental alertness, and provision of quality care. Some families were concerned about the lack of ethnic foods familiar to residents, and a few caregivers of African American and Afro-Caribbean residents requested more appropriate hair care for the residents and also asked for weekly Protestant services.

10. Staff behaviors that communicate care and empathy to residents and their relatives are especially helpful.

These actions on the part of nursing assistants and orderlies, as well as other paid staff and social work interns, were mentioned most frequently by

Latina/o caregivers, and their special significance to these families may reflect the cultural values of *familismo* and *personalismo*. Extremely demanding workloads are likely to make it more difficult for staff to offer this kind of support, but such efforts should be encouraged because they enhance the quality of life in nursing homes.

11. Recreational opportunities for residents should take into account their diverse cultural backgrounds.

Service providers need to learn about the interests of residents earlier in their lives in order to offer activities that will be valued by residents after they move into the nursing home.

12. Many caregivers in each ethnic group believed that the nursing home had met their expectations or was not as bad as they had expected.

Caregivers of twenty African American and Afro-Caribbean, eighteen Latina/o, and twelve Jewish residents clearly indicated that they believed that placement was the right thing to do or the best decision. It is important for service providers to validate the difficulty of the placement process and also to help residents and caregivers understand that adjustment and acceptance of the placement generally occur with time.

13. Before admission to the nursing home, some of the residents in each group had experienced changes in caregivers, often related to declining health of the caregiver or geographic relocation of a caregiver or resident.

Geographic relocation of residents when assistance prior to placement became necessary occurred for only a few residents, most often Latinos/as, several of whom had relatives in the New York area and also in Puerto Rico. Some of these residents had lived at least part of their later years outside the mainland United States, even if they had lived on the mainland earlier in their lives. Service providers need to be aware of the incidence and importance of the loss of relatives and friends that residents may face as their care needs increase.

14. Adaptation of Drachman and Ryan's stage-of-migration framework to the nursing home placement process provides a useful framework for identifying and understanding what each resident and involved relatives and friends experience before placement (premigration and departure), during the decision-making process and move into the nursing home (transit), and during adjustment to the home (resettlement).

This framework outlines a process in which the individual moves from the culture(s) within which he or she has lived outside of the nursing home, through a transitional period, and into the culture of the nursing home, a journey that may also mean a move into a new culture ethnically or racially. Service providers must remember that this is an ideological move as well as a physical one and that past experiences, values, and attitudes are still a part of the resident's life.

This chapter has summarized information about what some of the relatives and friends of residents at Acacia Nursing Home considered "especially helpful" assistance from staff, structural impediments to nursing home service delivery, national workforce issues, alternatives to nursing home placement, and the implications of this study's findings and relevant concepts in the literature for provision of racially and ethnically sensitive services.

The behavior described as "especially helpful" generally involved empathic service delivery, particularly on the part of CNAs and orderlies, but studies of nursing homes have identified trends that discourage warm, caring, service provision that enhances the quality of life of residents and their informal caregivers. Issues addressed in the literature include lack of quality care because of emphasis on profits and lack of staff training and adequate pay; difficulties in measuring or controlling quality of care; presence or absence of bureaucratization; inability of residents to repay; the home-versus-hospital dichotomy; the medicalized model of nursing home care; commodification of residents and staff; estrangement of residents from control over their lives; existence of different "worlds" and "places" of administrative staff, floor staff, and residents; the shift of nursing homes on a continuum toward the acute care hospital and away from home; loss of personal care floors and the addition of short-term subacute care; Medicare's prospective payment system; and the influence of multiple market factors.

Other concerns include recruitment of enough workers in the twenty-first century to meet the national need. Various strategies have been developed to address the shortage of CNAs, geriatric social workers, geriatric nurses and nurse practitioners, and medical geriatricians. Working conditions, particularly for paraprofessionals, who are often underpaid, overworked, and lacking benefits, constitute another major issue. A large number of these workers are women and members of racial and ethnic minority groups.

Structural lag continues to affect the development of alternatives to nursing home placement for frail older adults who prefer to remain in the community. Nursing home placement was the last resort for most of the residents and their caregivers in this study, and the need for viable alternatives to placement has not been addressed adequately in the United States. Many had an adequate informal support system that coordinated care with formal providers, but eventually they needed services that were not available to them outside of a nursing home.

The prevailing theme in this study is the need to understand the experiences of nursing home residents and their families from the perspective of their racial and ethnic backgrounds. Individuals within and across groups do share many experiences, but important differences also exist. Drachman and Ryan's stage-of-migration framework makes it clear that immigration and migration add a unique perspective to the lives of individuals who undergo migration experiences. Furthermore, their framework provides a useful approach to understanding nursing home placement as a sequence of life experiences involving premigration and departure from residence in the larger community, transit, and resettlement in the nursing home.

REFERENCES

Abel, E. (1991). *Who Cares for the Elderly? Public Policy and the Experiences of Adult Daughters*. Philadelphia: Temple University Press.

Albert, S. (1990). Caregiving as a cultural system: Conceptions of filial obligation and parental dependency in urban America. *American Anthropologist* 92:319–331.

Alecxih, L. (2001). The impact of sociodemographic change on the future of long-term care. *Generations* 25, no. 1: 7–11.

Andersen, M. and P. H. Collins. (2001). Shifting the Center and Reconstructing Knowledge. In M. Andersen and P. H. Collins, eds., *Race, Class, and Gender: An Anthology*, 11–19. Belmont, Calif.: Wadsworth.

Angel, D. and D. Hogan. (1994). The Demography of Minority Aging Populations. In *Minority Elders: Five Goals Toward Building a Public Policy Base*, 9–21. Report of the G.S.A. Task Force on Minority Issues in Gerontology. Washington, D.C.: Gerontological Society of America.

Angel, R. and J. Angel. (1997). *Who Will Care for Us? Aging and Long-Term Care in Multicultural America*. New York: New York University Press.

Ansak, M. (1990). The On Lok Model: Consolidating care and financing. *Generations* 14, no. 2: 73–74.

Antonucci, T. and H. Akiyama. (1991). Convoys of social support: Generational issues. *Marriage and Family Review* 16, nos. 1–2: 103–123.

Aranda, M. and B. Knight. (1997). The influence of ethnicity and culture on the caregiver stress and coping process: A sociocultural review and analysis. *Gerontologist* 37, no. 3: 342–353.

Archbold, P. (1983). An impact of parent-caring on women. *Family Relations* 32, no. 1: 39–45.

Atchley, R. (1994). *Social Forces and Aging*. Belmont, Calif.: Wadsworth.

Baca-Zinn, M. (1998). Feminist Rethinking from Racial-Ethnic Families. In S. Ferguson, ed., *Shifting the Center: Understanding Contemporary Families*, 12–21. Mountain View, Calif.: Mayfield.

Baca-Zinn, M. and B. Thornton-Dill. (1997). Theorizing Difference from Multiracial Feminism. In M. Baca-Zinn, P. Hondagneu-Sotelo, and M. Messner, eds., *Through the Prism of Difference: Readings on Sex and Gender*, 23–29. Boston: Allyn and Bacon.

Barresi, C. and D. Stull, eds. (1993). *Ethnic Elderly and Long-Term Care*. New York: Springer.

Barrett, A. and S. Lynch. (1999). Caregiving networks of elderly persons: Variation by marital status. *Gerontologist* 39, no. 6: 695–704.

Barusch, A., R. Greene, and J. Connelly. (1990). *Strategies for Increasing Gerontology Content in Social Work Education*. Washington, D.C.: Association for Gerontology in Higher Education.

Beckett, J. and D. Dungee-Anderson. (1992). Older Minorities: Asian, Black, Hispanic, and Native Americans. In R. Schneider and N. Kropf, eds., *Gerontological Social Work: Knowledge, Service Settings, and Special Populations*, 277–322. Chicago: Nelson-Hall.

Bell, J. (1996). Decision making in nursing home placement. *Journal of Women and Aging* 8, no. 1: 45–60.

———. (2001). Telephone interview, January 23.

Bengtson, V. and R. Harootyan. (1994). *Intergenerational Linkages: Hidden Connections in American Society*. New York: Springer.

Benjamin, A., R. Matthias, and T. Franke. (2000). Comparing consumer-directed and agency models for providing support services at home. *Health Services Research* 35, no. 1, pt. 2: 351–366.

Berg-Weger, M. (1996). *Caring for Elderly Parents: The Relationship Between Stress and Choice*. New York: Garland.

Berg-Weger, M. and D. Rubio. (1995). Role induction and caregiver strain: A structural equation approach. *Journal of Social Service Research* 21, no. 2: 33–53.

Blanchette, P. and B. Flynn. (2001). Geriatric medicine: An approaching crisis. *Generations* 25, no. 1: 80–84.

Bonder, B. (2001). Allied health workers and care for frail elders in the twenty-first century. *Generations* 25, no. 1: 76–78.

Bonder, B., L. Martin, and A. Miracle. (2001). Achieving cultural competence: The challenge for clients and healthcare workers in a multicultural society. *Generations* 25, no. 1: 35–42.

Braus, P. (1994). When Mom needs help. *American Demographics* 16, no. 3: 38–41.

Briggs, L. (1986). *Learning How to Ask*. Cambridge, Eng.: Canbridge University Press.

Brody, E. (1985). Parent care as a normative family stress. *Gerontologist* 25, no. 1: 19–29.

———. (1990). *Women in the Middle: Their Parent-Care Years*. New York: Springer.

Brody, E., C. Hoffman, and R. Winter. (1987). Family relationships of depressed, dysphoric, and nondepressed residents of nursing homes and senior housing.

Paper presented at the fortieth annual meeting of the Gerontological Society of America, Washington, D.C.

Brody, E., R. Pruchno, and N. Dempsey. (1989). Differential strains of sons and daughters of the institutionalized aged. Paper presented at the forty-second annual meeting of the Gerontological Society of America, Minneapolis.

Bumagin, V. and K. Hirn. (2001). *Caregiving: A Guide for Those Who Give Care and Those Who Receive It*. New York: Springer.

Burnley, C. (1992). Caregiving: The Impact of Emotional Support for Single Women. In T. Gubrium and K. Charmaz, eds., *Aging, Self, and Community: A Collection of Readings*, 117–128. Greenwich, Conn.: JAI Press.

Cancian, F. and S. Oliker. 2000. *Caring and Gender*. Walnut Creek, Calif.: AltaMira.

Cantor, M. (1979). Informal Support Systems of New York's Inner City Elderly: Is Ethnicity a Factor? In D. Gelfank and A. Kutzik, eds., *Ethnicity and Aging: Theory, Research, and Policy*, 153–174. New York: Springer.

———. (1983). Strain among caregivers: A study of experience in the United States. *Gerontologist* 23:579–604.

Chang, C. and S. White-Means. (1991). The men who care: An analysis of male primary caregivers who care for frail elderly at home. *Journal of Applied Gerontology* 10:343–358.

Chatters, L. and R. Taylor. (1993). Intergenerational Support: The Provision of Assistance to Parents by Adult Children. In J. Jackson, L. Chatters, and R. Taylor, eds., *Aging in Black America*, 69–83. Newbury Park, Calif.: Sage.

Cicirelli, V. (1981). Kin relationships of childless and one-child elderly in relation to social services. *Journal of Gerontological Social Work* 4, no. 1: 19–33.

———. (1992). *Family Caregiving: Autonomous and Paternalistic Decision Making*. Newbury Park, Calif.: Sage.

Coke, M. and J. Twaite. (1995). *The Black Elderly: Satisfaction and Quality of Later Life*. New York: Haworth.

Collins, C. and R. Jones. (1997). Emotional distress and morbidity in dementia carers: A matched comparison of husbands and wives. *Journal of Geriatric Psychiatry* 12:1168–1173.

Collins, P. (1991). *Black Feminist Thought: Knowledge, Consciousness, and the Politics of Empowerment*. London: Harper Collins.

———. (1997). The meaning of motherhood in black culture and black mother-daughter relationships. In M. Baca-Zinn, P. Hondagneu-Sotelo, and M. Messner, eds., *Through the Prism of Difference: Readings on Sex and Gender*, 264–275. Boston: Allyn and Bacon.

Connell, C. and G. Gibson. (1997). Racial, ethnic, and cultural differences in dementia caregiving: Review and analysis. *Gerontologist* 37, no. 3: 355–364.

Consortium of New York Geriatric Education Centers. (2001). *A Professional Training Program in Interdisciplinary Geriatrics and Gerontology: 2001–2002 Program*. New York: New York University School of Nursing.

Crown, W. (1994). A national profile of home care, nursing home, and hospital aides. *Generations* 18, no. 3: 29–33.

Csikszmentihayli, M. (1975). *Beyond Boredom and Anxiety*. San Francisco: Jossey-Bass.

Darnay, A. (1998). *Statistical Record of Health and Medicine*. Detroit: Gale Research.

Delgado, M. and S. Tennstedt. (1997). Puerto Rican sons as primary caregivers of elderly parents. *Social Work* 42, no. 2: 125–134.

Diamond, T. (1992). *Making Gray Gold: Narratives of Nursing Home Care*. Chicago: University of Chicago Press.

Diener, E., E. Suh, and S. Oishi. (1997). Recent findings on subjective well-being. *Indian Journal of Clinical Psychology* 24, no. 1: 25–41.

Dobrof, R. (1977). Part I. Guide to Practice. In R. Dobrof and E. Litwak, *Maintenance of Family Ties of Long-Term Care Patients: Theory and Guide to Practice*, 1–79. DHEW Publication no. (ADM) 77–400. Washington, D.C.: U.S. Government Printing Office.

Doty, P., M. Jackson, and W. Crown. (1998). The impact of female caregivers' employment status on patterns of formal and informal eldercare. *Gerontologist* 38, no. 3: 331–341.

Drachman, D. (1992). A stage-of-migration framework for service to immigrant populations. *Social Work* 37, no. 1: 68–72.

Drachman, D. and A. Ryan. (1991). Immigrants and Refugees. In A. Gitterman, ed., *Handbook of Social Work Practice with Vulnerable Populations*, 618–646. New York: Columbia University Press.

Dwyer, J., J. Henretta, R. Coward, and A. Barton. (1992). Changes in the helping behaviors of adult children as caregivers. *Research on Aging* 14, no. 3: 351–375.

Eckert, J. and S. Shulman. (1996). Daughters caring for their aging mothers: A midlife developmental process. *Journal of Gerontological Social Work* 25, no. 3/4: 17–32.

Espino, D. (1993). Hispanic Elderly and Long-Term Care: Implications for Ethnically Sensitive Services. In C. Barresi and D. Stull, eds., *Ethnic Elderly and Long-Term Care*, 101–112. New York: Springer.

Espino, D., R. Neufeld, M. Mulvihill, and L. Libow. (1988). Hispanic and non-Hispanic elderly on admission to the nursing home: A pilot study. *Gerontologist* 28, no. 6: 821–824.

Estes, C. and J. Swan. (1993). *The Long Term Care Crisis: Elders Trapped in the No-Care Zone*. Newbury Park, Calif.: Sage.

Facio, E. (1997). Chicanas and Aging: Toward Definitions of Womanhood. In J. Coyle, ed., *Handbook on Women and Aging*, 335–350. Westport, Conn.: Greenwood.

Fandetti, D. and J. Goldmeier. (1988). Social workers as culture mediators in health care settings. *Health and Social Work* 13 (Summer): 171–179.

Feder, J., H. Komisar, and M. Niefeld. (2000). Long-term care in the United States: An overview. *Health Affairs* 19, no. 3: 40–56.

Ferster, L. (2001). Telephone interview, December 30.

Finley, N., M. Roberts, and B. Banahan. (1988). Motivators and inhibitors of attitudes of filial obligation toward aging parents. *Gerontologist* 28, no. 1: 73–83.

Fitting, M., P. Rabins, M. Lucas, and J. Eastham. (1986). Caregivers for dementia patients: A comparison of husbands and wives. *Gerontologist* 26 (3): 248–252.

Fredriksen, K. (1996). Gender differences in employment and the informal care of adults. *Journal of Women and Aging* 8:35–53.

Fulmer, T., E. Flaherty, and L. Medley. (2001). Geriatric nurse practitioners: Vital to the future of healthcare for elders. *Generations* 25, no. 1: 72–75.

Garcia-Preto, N. (1996). Latino Families: An Overview. In M. McGoldrick, J. Giordano, and J. Pearce, eds., *Ethnicity and Family Therapy*, 141–154. New York: Guilford.

George, L. and L. Gwyther. (1986). Caregiver well-being: A multidimensional examination of family caregivers of demented adults. *Gerontologist* 26, no. 3: 253–259.

Gibson, R. (1982). African-Americans at middle and later life: Resources and coping. *Annals of the American Academy of Political and Social Science* 464:79–90.

Glenn, E. (1992). From servitude to service work: Historical continuities in the racial division of paid reproductive labor. *Signs* 18:1–43.

Glicksman, A. (1990). The new Jewish elderly. *Journal of Aging and Judaism* 5, no. 1: 7–22.

Goffman, E. (1961). *Asylums*. Garden City, N.Y.: Anchor.

Gorelick, P. (1994). Stroke prevention: An opportunity for efficient utilization of health care resources during the coming decade. *Stroke* 25: 220–224.

Greene, V. and J. Ondrich. (1990). Risk factors for nursing home admissions and exits: A discrete-time hazard function approach. *Journal of Gerontology, Social Sciences* 45 (6): S250–S258.

Gubrium, J. (1997). *Living and Dying at Murray Manor*. Charlottesville: University Press of Virginia.

Hagestad, G. (2000). The Family: Women and Grandparents as Kin-Keepers. In H. Moody, ed., *Aging: Concepts and Controversies*, 85–88. Thousand Oaks, Calif.: Pine Forge.

Haley, W., C. West, V. Wadley, G. Ford, F. White, J. Barrett, L. Harrell, and D. Roth. (1995). Psychological, social, and health impact of caregiving: A comparison of black and white dementia family caregivers and noncaregivers. *Psychology and Aging* 10:540–552.

Hanks, R. (1991). Intergenerational perspectives on family ethical dilemmas. *Marriage and Family Review* 16, nos. 1–2: 161–173.

Harmon, R. and R. Blieszner. (1990). Filial responsibility expectations among adult child–older parent pairs. *Journal of Gerontology* 45, no. 3: 110–112.

Harootyan, R. and R. Vorek. (1994). Volunteering, Helping, and Gift Giving in Families and Communities. In V. Bengtson and R. Harootyan, eds., *Intergenerational Linkages: Hidden Connections in American Society*, 77–111. New York: Springer.

Harris, P. (1998). Listening to caregiving sons: Misunderstood realities. *Gerontologist* 38, no. 3: 342–352.

Hazuda, H. and D. Espino. (1997). Aging, Chronic Disease, and Physical Disability in Hispanic Elderly. In K. Markides and M. Miranda, eds., *Minorities, Aging, and Health*, 127–148. Thousand Oaks, Calif.: Sage.

Henderson, J. (1995). The Culture of Care in a Nursing Home: Effects of a Medicalized Model of Long Term Care. In J. Henderson and M. Vesperi, eds., *The Culture of Long Term Care: Nursing Home Ethnography*, 37–54. Westport, Conn.: Bergin and Garvey.

Henderson, J. and M. Vesperi, eds. (1995). *The Culture of Long Term Care: Nursing Home Ethnography*. Westport, Conn.: Bergin and Garvey.

Hing, E. and B. Bloom. (1990). Long-term care for the functionally dependent elderly. *Vital and Health Statistics*, series 13, 104:31.

Holstein, M. (2001). Books: Voices seldom heard. Review of *Making Gray Gold: Narratives of Nursing Home Care*, by Timothy Diamond. *Generations* 25, no. 1: 92–94.

Horowitz, A. (1985a). Family Caregiving to the Frail Elderly. In C. Eisdorfer, ed., *Annual Review of Gerontology and Geriatrics*. Vol. 5. New York: Springer.

——. (1985b). Sons and daughters as caregivers to older parents: Differences in role performances and consequences. *Gerontologist* 25, no. 6: 612–617.

Hraba, J. (1994). *American Ethnicity*. Itasca: Peacock.

Hughes, S., A. Giobbie-Hurder, F. Weaver, J. Kubal, and W. Henderson. (1999). Relationship between caregiver burden and health-related quality of life. *Gerontologist* 39, no. 5: 534–545.

Ingersoll-Dayton, B., M. Starrels, and D. Dowler. (1996). Caregiving for parents and parents-in-law: Is gender important? *Gerontologist* 36, no. 4: 483–491.

John A. Hartford Foundation. (2001). Featured initiatives. http://www.jhartfound.org/fi.htm. Accessed February 5, 2002.

Johnson, C. (1983). Dyadic family relations and social support. *Gerontologist* 23, no. 4: 377–383.

——. (1985). *Growing Up and Growing Old in Italian-American Families*. New Brunswick, N.J.: Rutgers University Press.

Johnson, C. and D. Catalano. (1981). Childless elderly and their family supports. *Gerontologist* 21, no. 6: 610–618.

Johnson, C. and L. Grant. (1985). *The Nursing Home in American Society*. Baltimore: Johns Hopkins University Press.

Johnson, T., E. Hardt, and A. Kleinman. (1995). Cultural Factors in the Medical Interview. In M. Lipkin, S. Putnam, and A. Lazare, eds., *The Medical Interview: Clinical Care, Education, and Research*. New York: Springer-Verlag.

Jones, D. and G. van Amelsvoort Jones. (1986). Communication patterns between nursing staff and the ethnic elderly in a long-term-care facility. *Journal of Advanced Nursing* 11:265–272.

Jordan, J. (1991). The Meaning of Mutuality. In J. Jordan, A. Kaplan, J. Miller, I. Stiver, and J. Surrey, eds., *Women's Growth in Connection: Writings from the Stone Center*, 81–96. New York: Guilford.

Kaye, L. (1997). Informal Caregiving by Older Men. In J. Kosberg and L. Kaye, eds., *Elderly Men: Special Problems and Professional Challenges*, 231–349. New York: Springer.

Kaye, L. and J. Applegate. (1990). *Men as Caregivers to the Elderly: Understanding and Aiding Unrecognized Family Support*. Lexington, Mass.: Lexington Books.

———. (1994). Older Men and the Family Caregiving Orientation. In E. Thompson, Jr., ed., *Older Men's Lives*, 218–236. Thousand Oaks, Calif.: Sage.

Kolb, P. (1998). Trends in social services in nursing homes in the era of managed care. Paper presented at the annual meeting of the Gerontological Society of America, November 23, 1998.

———. (1999). A stage of migration approach to understanding nursing home placement in Latino families. *Journal of Multicultural Social Work* 7, no. 3/4: 95–112.

———. (2000). Continuing to care: Black and Latina daughters' assistance to their mothers in nursing homes. *Affilia* 15, no. 4: 502–525.

Kosberg, J. (1992). An International Perspective on Family Care of the Elderly: An Introductory Overview. In J. Kosberg, ed., *Family Care of the Elderly: Social and Cultural Changes*, 1–13. Newbury Park, Calif.: Sage.

Kovar, M. (1986). Aging in the eighties: Preliminary data from the Supplement on Aging to the National Health Income Survey, United States, January–June 1984. *Advance Data from Vital and Health Statistics*. 115 DHHS Pub. No. PHS 86–1250. Hyattsville, Md.: Public Health Service.

Kramer, B. and S. Kipnis. (1995). Eldercare and work-role conflict: Toward an understanding of gender differences in caregiver burden. *Gerontologist* 35, no. 3: 340–358.

Kramer, B. and J. Lambert. (1999). Caregiving as a life course transition among older husbands: A prospective study. *Gerontologist* 39, no. 6: 658–667.

Krause, A., L. Grant, and B. Long. (1999). Sources of stress reported by daughters of nursing home residents. *Journal of Aging Studies* 13, no. 3: 349–364.

Lacayo, C. (1993). Hispanic Elderly: Policy Issues in Long-Term Care. In C. Barresi and D. Stull, eds., *Ethnic Elderly and Long-term Care*, 223–234. New York: Springer.

Lemann, N. (1991). *The Promised Land: The Great Black Migration and How It Changed America*. New York: Vintage.

Leon, J. and S. Franco. (1998). *Home- and Community-Based Workforce*. Final report prepared for the Henry J. Kaiser Foundation. Bethesda: Project Hope.

Lubben, J. and R. Becerra. (1987). Social Support Among Black, Mexican, and Chinese Elderly. In D. Gelfand and R. Becerra, eds., *Research and Ethnic Dimensions of Aging*, 130–144. New York: Springer.

Manton, K. and B. Soldo. (1985). Dynamics of health changes in the oldest old: New perspectives and evidence. *Milbank Memorial Fund Quarterly Health and Society* 63, no. 2: 206–285.

McAuley, W. and J. Travis. (1997). Positions of influence in the nursing home admission decision. *Research on Aging* 19, no. 1: 26–45.

McGoldrick, M., J. Giordano, and J. Pearce, eds. (1996). *Ethnicity and Family Therapy*. New York: Guilford.

McGrew, K. (1991). *Daughters' Decision Making About the Nature and Level of Their Participation in the Long-Term Care of Their Dependent Elderly Mothers: A Qualitative Study*. Oxford, Ohio: Scripps Gerontology Center.

McLean, A. and M. Perkinson. (1995). The Head Nurse as Key Informant: How Beliefs and Institutional Pressures Can Structure Dementia Care. In J. Henderson and M. Vesperi, eds., *The Culture of Long Term Care: Nursing Home Ethnography*, 127–148. Westport, Conn.: Bergin and Garvey.

Midlarsky, E. (1994). Altruism Through the Life Course. In E. Kahana, D. Biegel, and M. Wykle, eds., *Family Caregiving Across the Lifespan*, 69–95. Thousand Oaks, Calif.: Sage.

Miller, B. (1990). Gender Differences in Spouse Management of the Caregiver Role. In E. Abel and M. Nelson, eds., *Circles of Care:Work and Identity in Women's Lives*, 92–104. Albany: State University of New York Press.

Miller, B. and L. Cafasso. (1992). Gender differences in caregiving: Fact or artifact? *Gerontologist* 32, no. 4: 498–507.

Miller, B. and S. McFall. (1991). Stability and change in the informal task support network of frail older persons. *Gerontologist* 31, no. 6: 735–745.

Mills, C. W. (1959). *The Sociological Imagination*. London: Oxford University Press.

Montgomery, R. (1992). Gender Differences in Patterns of Child-Parent Caregiving Relationships. In J. Dwyer and R. Coward, eds., *Gender, Families, and Elder Care*, 65–83. Newbury Park, Calif.: Sage.

Moody, H. (2002). *Aging: Concepts and Controversies*. Thousand Oaks, Calif.: Pine Forge.

Moreno, C. (2002). Telephone interview, January 28.

Morrison, B. (1979). Black aged in nursing homes: An application of the shared function thesis. Ph.D. diss., Columbia University School of Social Work, New York.

Motenko, A. (1988). Respite Care and Pride in Caregiving in the Experience of Six Older Men Caring for Their Disabled Wives. In S. Reinharr and G. Rowles, eds., *Qualitative Gerontology*, 104–127. New York: Springer-Verlag.

Mui, A. (1992). Caregiver strain among black and white daughter caregivers: A role theory perspective. *Gerontologist* 32, no. 2: 203–212.

———. (1995). Caring for frail elderly parents: A comparison of adult sons and daughters. *Gerontologist* 35, no. 1: 86–93.

Mui, A. and D. Burnette. (1994). Long-term care service use by frail elders: Is ethnicity a factor? *Gerontologist* 34, no. 2: 190–198.

Mui, A., N. Choi, and A. Monk. (1998). *Long-Term Care and Ethnicity*. Westport, Conn.: Auburn House.

National Alliance for Caregiving and the American Association of Retired Persons. (1997). *Family Caregiving in the U.S.: Findings from a National Survey*. Final Report. Bethedsa, Md.: National Alliance for Caregiving.

Neal, M., B. Ingersoll-Dayton, and M. Starrels. (1997). Gender and relationship differences in caregiving patterns and consequences among employed caregivers. *Gerontologist* 37, no. 6: 804–816.

Parks, S. and M. Pilusik. (1991). Caregiver burden: Gender and the psychological costs of caregiving. *American Journal of Orthopsychiatry* 61, no. 4: 501–509.

Peters-Davis, N., M. Moss, and R. Pruchno. (1999). Children-in-law in caregiving families. *Gerontologist* 39, no. 1: 66–75.

Peterson, D. (1990). Personnel to serve the aging in the field of social work: Implications for educating professionals. *Social Work* 35, no. 5: 412–415.

Pohl, J., C. Boyd, and B. Given. (1997). Mother-daughter relationships during the first year of caregiving: A qualitative study. *Journal of Women and Aging* 9, no. 1/2: 133–149.

Pollard, L. (1987). "Around the Verge of Parting Life": Hobart Jackson, the Stephen Smith Home, and Black Gerontology. In R. Dobrof, ed., *Ethnicity and Gerontological Social Work*, 21–38. New York: Haworth.

Portes, A. and R. Rumbaut. (1996). *Immigrant America: A Portrait*. Berkeley: University of California Press.

Premo, T. (1984–1985). "A blessing to our declining years." Feminine responses to filial duty in the new republic. *International Journal of Aging and Human Development* 20: 69–74.

Reddy, M., ed. (1993). *Statistical Record of Hispanic Americans*. Detroit: Gale Research.

Rempusheski, M. (1989). The role of ethnicity in elder care. *Nursing Clinics of North America* 24, no. 3: 717–724.

Rhoades, J. and N. Krauss. (1999). *Nursing Home Trends, 1987 and 1906*. Rockville, Md.: U.S. Agency for Health Care Policy and Research.

Riley, M. (1986). The dynamisms of life stages: Roles, people, and age. *Human Development* 29, no. 3: 150–156.

———. (1987). On the significance of age in sociology. *American Sociological Review* 52:1–14.

———. (1994a). Changing lives and changing social structures: Common concerns of social science and public health. *American Journal of Public Health* 84, no. 8: 1214–1217.

———. (1994b). Aging and society: Past, present, and future. *Gerontologist* 34, no. 4: 436–446.

———, ed. (1979). *Aging from Birth to Death: Interdisciplinary Perspectives.* Boulder: Westview.

———, ed. (1988). *Social Change and the Life Course.* Beverly Hills, Calif.: Sage.

Riley, M., A. Foner, and J. Riley. (1999). The Aging and Society Paradigm. In V. Bengtson and K. W. Schaie, eds., *Handbook of Theories of Aging*, 327–343. New York: Springer.

Riley, M., R. Kahn, and A. Foner, eds. (1994). *Age and Structural Lag: Society's Failure to Provide Meaningful Opportunities in Work, Family, and Leisure.* New York: Wiley.

Riley, M. and J. Riley. (1986). Longevity and social structure: The added years. *Daedalus* 115, no. 1: 51–75.

Robinson, B. and M. Thurnher. (1979). Taking care of aged parents: A family cycle transition. *Gerontologist* 19, no. 5: 586–593.

Rose-Rego, S., M. Strauss, and K. Smyth. (1998). Differences in the perceived well-being of wives and husbands caring for persons with Alzheimer's disease. *Gerontologist* 38, no. 2: 224–230.

Rosen, A. and T. Persky. (1997). Meeting the mental health needs of older people: Policy and practice issues for social work. In C. Saltz, ed., *Social Work Response to the 1995 White House Conference on Aging: From Issues to Actions.* New York: Haworth.

Rosen, A. and J. Zlotnik. (2001). Social work's response to the growing older population. *Generations* 25, no. 1: 69–71.

Saldov, M. (1992). Communication needs of the ethnic elderly in hospitals and nursing homes. *Journal of Multicultural Social Work* 2, no. 2: 1–9.

Saldov, M. and P. Chow. (1994). The ethnic elderly in metro Toronto hospitals, nursing homes, and homes for the aged: Communication and health care. *International Journal of Aging and Human Development* 8, no. 2: 117–135.

Savishinsky, J. (1991). *The Ends of Time: Life and Work in a Nursing Home.* New York: Bergin and Garvey.

Schulz, R. and G. Williamson. (1991). A two-year longitudinal study of depression among Alzheimer's caregivers. *Psychology and Aging* 6, no. 4: 569–578.

Selig, S., T. Tomlinson, and T. Hickey. (1991). Ethical dimensions of intergenerational reciprocity: Implications for practice. *Gerontologist* 31, no. 5: 624–630.

Seltzer, M. and L. Li. (2000). The dynamics of caregiving: Transitions during a three-year prospective study. *Gerontologist* 40, no. 2: 165–178.

Shanas, E. (1969). The family as a social support system in old age. *Gerontologist* 9, no. 2: 169–174.

———. (1979). Social myth as hypothesis: The case of the family relations of old people. *Gerontologist* 19, no. 1: 3–9.

Shanas, E., P. Townsend, D. Wedderburn, H. Friis, P. Milhoj, and J. Stehouwer. (1968). *Old People in Three Industrial Societies.* New York: Atherton.

Shenk, D. (2001). *The Forgetting Alzheimer's: Portrait of an Epidemic*. New York: Doubleday.

Shield, R. (1988). *Uneasy Endings: Daily Life in an American Nursing Home*. Ithaca: Cornell University Press.

Silverstein, M., L. Lawton, and V. Bengtson. (1994). Types of relations between parents and adult children. In V. Bengtson and R. Harootyan, eds., *Intergenerational Linkages: Hidden Connections in American Society*, 43–76. New York: Springer.

Sleek, S. (1998). Psychology's cultural competence: Once "simplistic," now broadening. *APA Monitor* 29, no. 12: 1, 27.

Soldo, B. and K. Manton. (1985). Health status and service needs of the oldest old: Current patterns and future trends. *Milbank Memorial Fund Quarterly / Health and Society* 63:286–319.

Speaking from Experience: Nursing Assistants Share Their Knowledge of Dementia Care. Brooklyn: Cobble Hill Health Center.

Stoller, E. (1990). Males as helpers: The role of sons, relatives, and friends. *Gerontologist* 30, no. 2: 228–235.

Stoller, E. and R. Gibson. (1994). *Worlds of Difference: Inequality in the Aging Experience*. Thousand Oaks, Calif.: Pine Forge.

Stone, R. (2001). Research on frontline workers in long-term care. *Generations* 25, no. 1: 49–57.

Stone, R. and J. Wiener. (2001). *Who Will Care for Us? Addressing the Long Term Care Workforce Crisis*. Washington, D.C.: Urban Institute and the American Association of Homes and Services for the Aging.

Stone, R. L., L. Cafferata, and J. Sangl. (1987). Caregivers of the frail elderly: A national profile. *Gerontologist* 27, no. 5: 616–626.

Straw, L., S. O'Bryant, and D. Meddaugh. (1991). Support system participation in spousal caregiving: Alzheimer's disease versus other illnesses. *Journal of Applied Gerontology* 10, no. 3: 359–371.

Strawbridge, W., M. Wallhagen, S. Shema, and G. Kaplan. (1997). New burdens or more of the same? Comparing grandparent, spouse, and adult-child caregivers. *Gerontologist* 37, no. 4: 505–510.

Sue, S. (2000). The provision of effective mental health treatment by service providers. Paper presented at the National Institutes of Health conference, Toward Higher Levels of Analysis: Progress and Promise in Research on Social and Cultural Dimensions of Health, Bethesda, Maryland.

Surrey, J. (1991). The Self-in-Relation: A Theory of Women's Development. In J. Jordan, A. Kaplan, J. Miller, I. Stiver, and J. Surrey, eds., *Women's Growth in Connection: Writings from the Stone Center*, 51–66. New York: Guilford.

Tennstedt, S., S. Crawford, and J. McKinlay. (1993). Determining the pattern of community care: Is coresidence more important than caregiver relationship? *Journal of Gerontology: Social Sciences* 48, no. 2: S74–S83.

Thornton, N., S. White-Means, and H. Choi. (1993). Sociodemographic correlates of the size and composition of informal caregiver networks among frail ethnic elderly. *Journal of Comparative Family Studies* 24, no. 2: 235–250.

Tisdale, Sallie. (1987). *Harvest Moon: Portrait of a Nursing Home.* New York: Holt.

Toseland, R. and G. Smith. (1991). Family caregivers of the frail elderly. In A. Gitterman, ed., *Handbook of Social Work Practice with Vulnerable Populations,* 549–583. New York: Columbia University Press.

Townsend, A., C. Deimling, and L. Noelker. (1988). Transition to nursing home care: Sources of stress and family members' mental health. Paper presented at the forty-first annual meeting of the Gerontological Society of America, San Francisco.

Trilla, F. (1982). The plight of the elderly Puerto Rican. *Journal of Latin Community Health* 1:89–91.

Trotter, J. (1991). *The Great Migration in Historical Perspective: New Dimensions of Race, Class, and Gender.* Bloomington: Indiana University Press.

Turner, C. (1997). Clinical applications of the Stone Center theoretical approach to minority women. In J. Jordan, ed., *Women's Growth in Diversity: More Writings from the Stone Center,* 74–90. New York: Guilford.

Turner, V. (1967). *The Forest of Symbols.* Ithaca: Cornell University Press.

U.S. Bureau of the Census. (1993). *An Aging World II.* International Population Reports. P95/92–3. Washington, D.C.: U.S. Government Printing Office.

———. (1996). *65+ in the United States.* Current Population Reports, Special Studies. P23–190. Washington, D.C.: U.S. Government Printing Office.

———. (1997). *Statistical Abstract of the United States: 1997.* 117th ed. Washington, D.C.: U.S. Government Printing Office.

———. (1998). MS-1. Marital status of the population 15 years and over, by sex and race: 1950 to present. http://www.census.gov/p...edemo/ms-la/tabms-1.txt.

U.S. Bureau of Labor Statistics. (1998a). Employment projections. Civilian labor force by sex, age, race, and Hispanic origin, 1986, 1996, and projected 2006. http://stats.bls.gov/news.release/ecopro.table1.htm.

———. (1998b). Labor Force Statistics from the Current Population Survey. Table 2. Families by presence and relationship of employed members and family type, 1996–97 annual averages. http://www.bls.gov/news.release/famee.to2.htm.

———. (1998–1999). *Occupational Outlook Handbook.* Washington, D.C.: U.S. Department of Labor.

———. (2000). The employment situation: May 2000. *United States Department of Labor News.* Washington, D.C.: U.S. Department of Labor.

Vladeck, B. (1980). *Unloving Care: The Nursing Home Tragedy.* New York: Basic Books.

Wallace, S. (1990). Race versus class in the health care of African-American elderly. *Social Problems* 37, no. 4: 517–534.

Walter, C. (1991). Adult daughters and mothers: Stress in the caregiving relationship. *Journal of Women and Aging* 3, no. 3: 39–58.

Weisberg, J. (1983). Raising the self-esteem of mentally impaired nursing home residents. *Social Work* 28, no. 2: 163–164.

Westat, Inc. (1989). *Final Report to the Commonwealth Fund Commission on Elderly People Living Alone*. Rockville, Md.: Westat.

Wykle, M. and B. Kaskel. (1994). Increasing the longevity of minority older adults through improved health status. In *Minority Elders: Five Goals Toward Building a Public Policy Base*, 32–39. Report of the G.S.A. Task Force on Minority Issues in Gerontology. Washington, D.C.: Gerontological Society of America.

Yee, J. and R. Schulz. (2000). Gender differences in psychiatric morbidity among family caregivers: A review and analysis. *Gerontologist* 40, no. 2: 147–164.

Yeo, G. (1993). Ethnicity and Nursing Homes: Factors Affecting Use and Successful Components for Culturally Sensitive Care. In C. Barresi and D. Stull, eds., *Ethnic Elderly and Long-Term Care*, 161–177. New York: Springer.

Young, R. and E. Kahana. (1989). Specifying caregiver outcomes: Gender and relationship aspects of caregiving strain. *Gerontologist* 29, no. 5: 660–666.

Zarit, S., P. Todd, and J. Zarit. (1986). Subjective burden of husbands and wives of caregivers: A longitudinal study. *Gerontologist* 26, no. 3: 260–266.

INDEX